Danyeol Moon

English FLY HIGH

 Check in

Global Culture Center

English Fly High
Check in

Copyright © 2015 by Global Culture Center
All rights reserved.

No part of this publication may be reproduced,
stored in a retrieval system, or transmitted in any form or by any means,
electronic, mechanical, photocopying, recording, or otherwise,
without the prior permission of the publisher.

Global Culture Center
www.global21.co.kr
3rd Floor, 577-11, Siheung-daero, Guro-gu, Seoul, Republic of Korea
Tel. 02) 6365 – 5169
Fax. 02) 6365 – 5179

English Fly High - Check in
Author | Danyeol Moon
Publisher | Sooyeon Lee

Printed in Seoul,
4th Printing - Nov. 2019

ISBN 978-89-8233-252-4 14740
       978-89-8233-250-0 14740 (SET)

About this book

Language learning is like flying an airplane. The first thing that you should do is be equipped with vocabulary and grammar, with which you can assemble the airplane you will eventually fly. The next step is taking off where you will need a huge amounts of energy and practical skills along with courage and a certain degree of concentration and commitment. These primary steps not only need to be carried out with patience on the students' side but also be accompanied with a well-prepared and carefully designed course from the teachers' side. The next step is to fly high with the constant fueling of conversational topics and motivation to the final destination of the proficiency that is required in most standardized spoken tests and interviews of the times. These series of books provide all that is required for the preparation of the flight, guiding the students to acquire the essential volume of vocabulary and expressions and having them internalize the expressions immediately. It also helps students take off into the air, allowing them to actually utilize what they have learned in the previous steps in order for them to get ready for the real-life situations that they will be facing outside of classes. Finally, this series of books will provide them with the essential topics and high-level skills that are crucial in winning a competitive edge in business, as well as in academic pursuits. I hope that everyone who studies with these books will finally be at the destinations that they have been dreaming of.

Danyeol Moon

Contents

Unit	Title	Topic	Function	Grammar
Unit 1 Page 10	Is He Good-looking?	Appearances	- Describing Appearances - Talking about How People Look	- Be + Descriptive Adjectives - Or Questions
Unit 2 Page 18	What Are You Doing?	Everyday Activities	- Talking about What Activities Take Place	- Present Continuous (Be + Base verb + ing)
Unit 3 Page 26	This Shirt Is on Sale Today.	Shopping for Clothing	- Kinds of Clothing - Shopping for Clothing	- This, These, That, Those + Singular/Plural Nouns
Unit 4 Page 34	Do You Have a Brother?	Family Members	- Giving Information about Your Family - Talking about Age	- Have/Has - Cardinal Numbers
Unit 5 Page 42	I Go Bungee Jumping on Saturdays.	Days and Months	- Talking about Days, Dates, and Months - Habitual Actions	- It (pronoun) - What + Noun + Be + It? - Prepositions of Time (on, in, at) - Ordinal Numbers

Unit	Title	Topic	Function	Grammar
Unit 6 Page 50	My Favorite Sport Is Soccer.	Hobbies and Tastes	- Talking about What You Enjoy - Asking and Answering about Your Favorite Things	- Like + Noun - What kind of + Noun + do you like? - What is your favorite + Noun?
Unit 7 Page 58	I Usually Drink Coffee Five Times a Day.	Frequencies	- Describing the Frequency of Actions	- Frequency Adverbs - Subject + Be + Frequency Adverbs - The Number of Times
Unit 8 Page 66	It's Raining a Lot Today.	Weather Likes and Dislikes	- Describing Weather in Various Cities - Taking about What You Want to Do	- Want to + Base verb - It (Pronoun: Impersonal Subject) + Adjectives about Weather
Unit 9 Page 74	Can You Ride a Bicycle?	Talents and Abilities	- Expressing People's Talents and Abilities	- Can (Ability) + Base verb - Be Good at + Noun / ~ing
Unit 10 Page 82	Can I Have French fries?	Permission and Request	- Expressing Permission and Request - Expressing Obligation	- Can (Permission) + Base verb - Have to/Has to

Answers	Page 90
Appendixes	Page 102

Introduction

1. Words

Each Unit has a list of words that are essential to composition of the sentences key to the objective topics and functions of the unit.

2. Grammar

Grammar is crucial even in a conversation book because it is like the iron beams in a building which sustains and stabilizes the whole structure. So this book makes sure that the students, especially Korean adult students who need to comprehend the structure of the sentences that they are supposed to speak before they actually start using them through abundant examples and exercises.

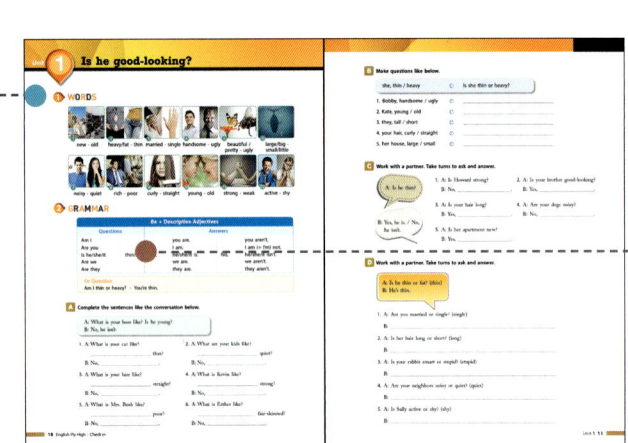

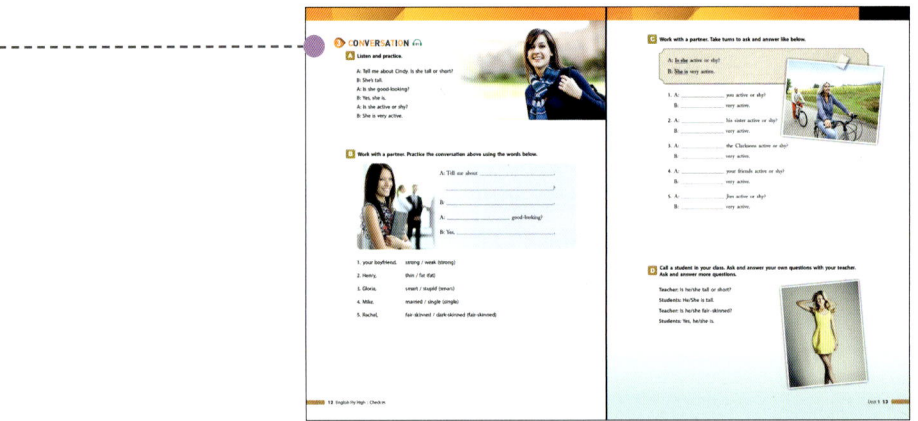

3. Conversation

Conversation exercises have been written based on the principles that the students are fully informed of the context of the interactive language settings and be well-equipped with multi-intelligence based input as well as repetitious practical output performance. Four steps of exercises (A-B-C-D) will help the students gradually and practically build their speaking skills without running out of conversational ideas and expressions. These exercises are easy but they will lead the learners to the objectives of the unit which in most cases means they have fully achieved the comprehension of the grammatical elements and the proficiency in speaking of the target objectives.

4. Reading

Reading must be pleasurable. It means that it shouldn't give ESL students any hard time going on and off the text looking up the dictionary and wrestling with the meaning of the article. It should be smooth and helpful to reminding and reinforcing of the things that they have newly acquired in the unit. The reading part in this book carries all the features that are portrayed here above. You will enjoy and you will learn!

Out to the world with Mr. Moon!

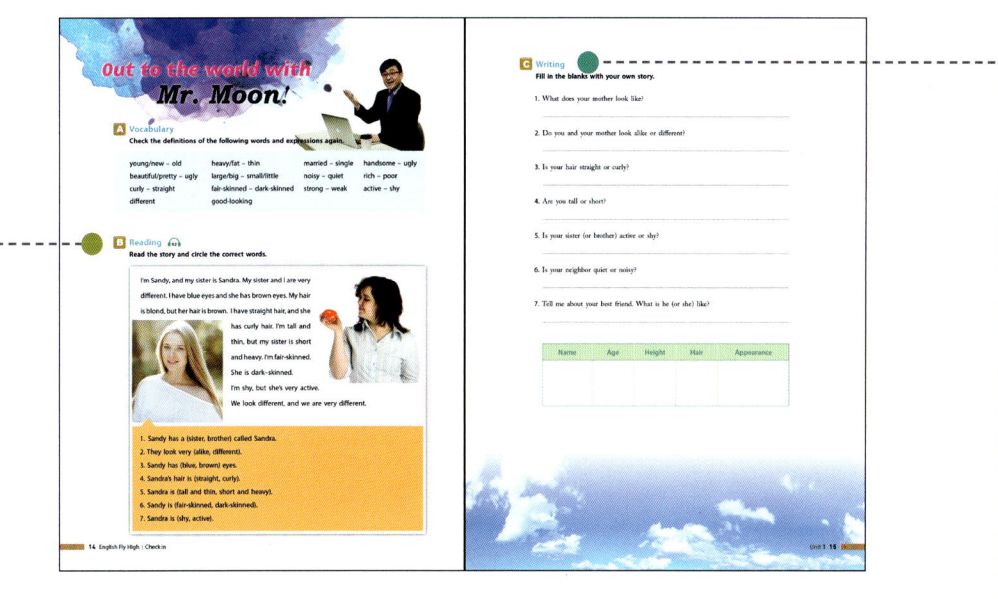

5. Writing

Reception is about mobility where production is about fruitfulness, meaning that even if you got free in understanding most of the language that are used in the unit, if you are not able to speak or write it on your own, you will end up not being capable of doing anything 'fruitful' to yourself. In most volumes of these books. This 'production' part is for speaking. But at the basic level (Packing / Check in) writing substitutes for the speaking for accuracy in knowing was considered more important than fluency.

Unit 1

Is He Good-looking?

LESSON PLAN

1) Topic
- Appearances

2) Function
- Describing Appearances
- Talking about How People Look

3) Grammar
- Be + Descriptive Adjectives
- Or Questions

Unit 1 Is he good-looking?

1 WORDS

 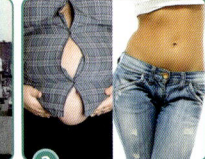 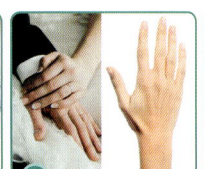   

1. new - old
2. heavy/fat - thin
3. married - single
4. handsome - ugly
5. beautiful/pretty - ugly
6. large/big - small/little

    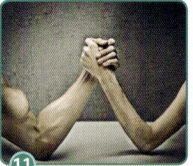 

7. noisy - quiet
8. rich - poor
9. curly - straight
10. young - old
11. strong - weak
12. active - shy

2 GRAMMAR

Be + Descriptive Adjectives					
Questions		**Answers**			
Am I Are you Is he/she/it Are we Are they	thin?	Yes,	you are. I am. he/she/it is. we are. they are.	No,	you aren't. I am (= I'm) not. he/she/it isn't. we aren't. they aren't.

Or Question
Am I thin or heavy? - You're thin.

A Complete the sentences like the conversation below.

> A: What is your boss like? Is he young?
> B: No, he isn't.

1. A: What is your cat like?
   _____ thin?
   B: No, _____.

2. A: What are your kids like?
   _____ quiet?
   B: No, _____.

3. A: What is your hair like?
   _____ straight?
   B: No, _____.

4. A: What is Kevin like?
   _____ strong?
   B: No, _____.

5. A: What is Mrs. Bush like?
   _____ poor?
   B: No, _____.

6. A: What is Esther like?
   _____ fair-skinned?
   B: No, _____.

B Make questions like below.

> she, thin / heavy → Is she thin or heavy?

1. Bobby, handsome / ugly → _____
2. Kate, young / old → _____
3. they, tall / short → _____
4. your hair, curly / straight → _____
5. her house, large / small → _____

C Work with a partner. Take turns to ask and answer.

> A: Is he thin?
> B: Yes, he is. / No, he isn't.

1. A: Is Howard strong?
   B: No, _____.

2. A: Is your brother good-looking?
   B: Yes, _____.

3. A: Is your hair long?
   B: Yes, _____.

4. A: Are your dogs noisy?
   B: No, _____.

5. A: Is her apartment new?
   B: Yes, _____.

D Work with a partner. Take turns to ask and answer.

> A: Is he thin or fat? (thin)
> B: He's thin.

1. A: Are you married or single? (single)

   B: _____

2. A: Is her hair long or short? (long)

   B: _____

3. A: Is your rabbit smart or stupid? (stupid)

   B: _____

4. A: Are your neighbors noisy or quiet? (quiet)

   B: _____

5. A: Is Sally active or shy? (shy)

   B: _____

3 CONVERSATION

A Listen and practice. 🎧 01

A: Tell me about Cindy. Is she tall or short?
B: She's tall.
A: Is she good-looking?
B: Yes, she is.
A: Is she active or shy?
B: She is very active.

B Work with a partner. Practice the conversation above using the words below.

A: Tell me about _____.
   _____?
B: _____.
A: _____ good-looking?
B: Yes, _____.

1. your boyfriend,   strong / weak (strong)

2. Henry,   thin / fat (fat)

3. Gloria,   smart / stupid (smart)

4. Mike,   married / single (single)

5. Rachel,   fair-skinned / dark-skinned (fair-skinned)

C Work with a partner. Take turns to ask and answer like below.

A: <u>Is she</u> active or shy?
B: <u>She is</u> very active.

1. A: _____ you active or shy?
   B: _____ very active.

2. A: _____ his sister active or shy?
   B: _____ very active.

3. A: _____ the Clarksons active or shy?
   B: _____ very active.

4. A: _____ your friends active or shy?
   B: _____ very active.

5. A: _____ Jim active or shy?
   B: _____ very active.

D Call a student in your class. Ask and answer your own questions with your teacher. Ask and answer more questions.

Teacher: Is **he/she** tall or short?

Students: **He/She** is tall.

Teacher: Is **he/she** fair-skinned?

Students: Yes, **he/she** is.

Unit 1 13

Out to the world with Mr. Moon!

A Vocabulary

Check the definitions of the following words and expressions again.

young/new – old	heavy/fat – thin	married – single	handsome – ugly
beautiful/pretty – ugly	large/big – small/little	noisy – quiet	rich – poor
curly – straight	fair-skinned – dark-skinned	strong – weak	active – shy
different	good-looking		

B Reading

Read the story and circle the correct words.

I'm Sandy, and my sister is Sandra. My sister and I are very different. I have blue eyes and she has brown eyes. My hair is blond, but her hair is brown. I have straight hair, and she has curly hair. I'm tall and thin, but my sister is short and heavy. I'm fair-skinned. She is dark–skinned. I'm shy, but she's very active. We look different, and we are very different.

1. Sandy has a (sister, brother) named Sandra.
2. They look very (alike, different).
3. Sandy has (blue, brown) eyes.
4. Sandra's hair is (straight, curly).
5. Sandra is (tall and thin, short and heavy).
6. Sandy is (fair-skinned, dark-skinned).
7. Sandra is (shy, active).

C Writing

Fill in the blanks with your own story.

1. What does your mother look like?
   _____

2. Do you and your mother look alike or different?
   _____

3. Is your hair straight or curly?
   _____

4. Are you tall or short?
   _____

5. Is your sister (or brother) active or shy?
   _____

6. Is your neighbor quiet or noisy?
   _____

7. Tell me about your best friend. What is he (or she) like?
   _____

Name	Age	Height	Hair	Appearance

Unit 2

What Are You Doing?

LESSON PLAN

1 Topic
- Everyday Activities

2 Function
- Talking about What Activities Take Place

3 Grammar
- Present Continuous (Be + Base verb + ing)

Unit 2 — What are you doing?

1 WORDS

1. cooking
2. drinking
3. driving
4. eating
5. listening
6. playing
7. reading
8. singing
9. sleeping
10. studying
11. swimming
12. watching
13. working

2 GRAMMAR

Present Continuous (Be + Base verb + ing)			
Statements		**Questions**	
I'm You're He's/She's/It's We're They're	working.	Am I Are you Is he/she/it Are we Are they	working?
Short Answers			
Yes,	you are. I am. he/she/it is. we are. they are.	No,	you aren't. I'm not. he/she/it isn't. we aren't. they aren't.

A Complete the sentences.

> I'm working (work) now.

1. We _____ (read) a book.
2. She _____ (drink) milk.
3. They _____ (watch) TV.
4. He _____ (eat) breakfast.
5. You _____ (study) English.

B Work with a partner. Take turns to ask and answer like below.

> A: you → B: What are you doing?

1. A: we → B: _____?
2. A: she → B: _____?
3. A: they → B: _____?
4. A: he → B: _____?
5. A: I → B: _____?

C Work with a partner. Take turns to ask and answer.

> A: What are you doing?
> B: I'm working.

1. A: _____ Tom doing?
   B: _____ (read) the newspaper.

2. A: _____ you and your sister doing?
   B: _____ (watch) TV.

3. A: _____ Martha doing?
   B: _____ (cook) spaghetti.

4. A: _____ your classmates doing?
   B: _____ (study) English.

5. A: _____ Gary doing?
   B: _____ (drive) a car.

6. A: _____ the boys doing?
   B: _____ (play) basketball.

D Work with a partner. Take turns to ask and answer the questions on your own.

> A: Where are you?
> B: I'm in the classroom.
> A: What are you doing?
> B: I'm studying English.

> A: Where is your mother?
> B: She's at home.
> A: What is she doing?
> B: She's cooking.

A: Where are you?
B: I'm _____.
A: What are you doing?
B: I'm _____.

A: Where is your mother?
B: She's _____.
A: What is she doing?
B: She's _____.

3 CONVERSATION

A Listen and practice.

A: Where's Daniel?
B: He's in the dining room.
A: What's he doing?
B: He's eating breakfast.
A: And is he reading the newspaper?
B: Yes, he is.

B Work with a partner. Practice the conversation above using the words below.

A: Where _____?

B: _____ in the _____.

A: What _____ doing?

B: _____.

1. Lisa, kitchen, cook dinner

2. you, living room, listen to music

3. Henry and his friends, yard, play basketball

4. Susan, dining room, drink milk

5. Jane, park, talk on the phone

6. you and Judy, restaurant, eat lunch

C Work with a partner. Take turns to practice a conversation.

work / sleep

A: Is Juliet working?

B: No, she isn't. She's sleeping now.

① sleep / eat fish

A: _____ your cat _____?

B: No, _____. _____ now.

② study / take a shower

A: _____ Karen _____?

B: No, _____. _____ now.

③ swim / play the guitar

A: _____ Jim _____?

B: No, _____. _____ now.

④ work / play cards

A: _____ they _____?

B: No, _____. _____ now.

⑤ dance / sing

A: _____ the girls _____?

B: No, _____. _____ now.

D Play a miming game. Take turns to mime an action. The class tries to guess what he(she) is doing. Here are some ideas.

Teacher: What is he/she doing?

Class: He's/She's dancing. Are you dancing?

Miming student: Yes, I am. / No, I'm not.
I'm swimming.

Unit 2 21

Out to the world with Mr. Moon!

A Vocabulary

Check the definitions of the following words and expressions again.

cooking	drinking	driving	eating	listening
playing	reading	singing	sleeping	studying
swimming	watching	working	talking on the phone	

B Reading

Read the story and answer the questions.

Jimmy and his friends are at the beach now. It's a nice day. What are they doing? Jimmy is reading a book. Beth and her dog are sleeping. Ken is playing the guitar. Grace is listening to music. Lon is swimming in the water. Alice is eating a sandwich. Some boys around them are playing beach volleyball. Jimmy and his friends are happy. Everyone is having a good time at the beach.

1. Where are Jimmy and his friends?
2. How's the weather?
3. What is Jimmy doing?
4. Are Beth and her dog sleeping?
5. What is Ken doing?
6. Is Lon talking on the phone?
7. What is Alice doing?
8. What are the boys around them doing?

C Writing

Patty and her friends are in the park today. Using this picture, write a story about them.

Patty	Alex	Jenny
cat	Jason	Rosa

Unit 3

This Shirt Is on Sale Today.

LESSON PLAN

1) Topic
- Shopping for Clothing

2) Function
- Kinds of Clothing
- Shopping for Clothing

3) Grammar
- This, These, That, Those + Singular/Plural Nouns

Unit 3 — This shirt is on sale today.

1 WORDS

1. belt
2. blouse
3. boots
4. coat
5. dress
6. earrings
7. glasses
8. gloves
9. hat
10. jacket
11. jeans
12. pajamas
13. pants
14. purse
15. shirt
16. shoes
17. skirt
18. socks
19. sweater
20. tie

2 GRAMMAR

This, These, That, Those + Singular/Plural Nouns	
Singular	**Plural**
This is a shirt.	These are shirts.
That is a shirt.	Those are shirts.
This shirt is on sale.	These shirts are on sale.
That shirt is on sale.	Those shirts are on sale.

Pronunciations of Plural Nouns

[s]: shirts, hats, coats (most nouns)
[z]: shoes, jeans, gloves (nouns ending in a, e, i, o, u, l, m, n, r)
[iz]: blouses, boxes, watches (nouns ending in s, x, z, sh, ch)

A Make [s], [z], [iz] lists.

| boots | dresses | earrings | glasses | jackets | jeans |
| pajamas | pants | purses | shoes | skirts | socks | sweaters |

[s]	[z]	[iz]
shirts	gloves	blouses

26 English Fly High | Check in

B Circle the correct words.

1. (This, These) is a nice blouse.
2. I like (that, those) gloves.
3. Is (this, these) sweater expensive?
4. (That, Those) are my jeans.
5. Are (this, these) your earrings?

C Work with a partner. Take turns to ask and answer.

A: How about this? This shirt is on sale today.
B: How about that? I like that shirt.

1. boots
   A: How about _____? _____ on sale today.
   B: How about _____? I like _____.

2. hat
   A: How about _____? _____ on sale today.
   B: How about _____? I like _____.

3. glasses
   A: How about _____? _____ on sale today.
   B: How about _____? I like _____.

4. coat
   A: How about _____? _____ on sale today.
   B: How about _____? I like _____.

D What are you wearing today? What are the students in your class wearing today? Take turns to tell what you're wearing. Here is a model conversation.

> A: What are you wearing?
> B: I'm wearing this shirt, these blue jeans, and these glasses.
> A: What is the teacher wearing?
> B: She's wearing that blouse, that skirt, and those earrings.

A: What are you wearing?
B: I'm wearing this _____, these _____ and these _____.
A: What is the teacher wearing?
B: She's/He's wearing that _____, that _____ and those _____.

Unit 3 27

3 CONVERSATION

A Listen and practice. 🎧 05

A: May I help you?
B: Yes, please. I'm looking for a shirt.
A: How about this? This shirt is on sale today.
B: I like that shirt. Is that on sale, too?
A: Yes, it's half price.

B Work with a partner. Practice the conversation above using the words below.

> A: May I help you?
> B: Yes, please. I'm looking for _____.
> A: How about _____? _____ on sale today.
> B: I like _____. _____ on sale, too?

1
pants

A: May I help you?
B: Yes, please. I'm looking for _____.
A: How about _____? _____ on sale today.
B: I like _____. _____ on sale, too?

2
belt

A: May I help you?
B: Yes, please. I'm looking for _____.
A: How about _____? _____ on sale today.
B: I like _____. _____ on sale, too?

3
shoes

A: May I help you?
B: Yes, please. I'm looking for _____.
A: How about _____? _____ on sale today.
B: I like _____. _____ on sale, too?

4
jacket

A: May I help you?
B: Yes, please. I'm looking for _____.
A: How about _____? _____ on sale today.
B: I like _____. _____ on sale, too?

5
socks

A: May I help you?
B: Yes, please. I'm looking for _____.
A: How about _____? _____ on sale today.
B: I like _____. _____ on sale, too?

C Work with a partner. Have a conversation using the sentences below.

A: Is this shirt on sale?

B: Yes, it's a steal.

A: Are these glasses on sale, too?

B: Yes, they're half price.

1. skirt / socks

2. tie / dresses

3. purse / hats

4. suit / sweaters

5. blouse / jeans

D What clothes and things are there in your classroom? Each student gives some things to the teacher: for example, bags, pencils, cell phones, pencil cases, lipsticks, glasses. Pretend you're shopping at a store using the conversation below.

A: May I help you?

B: Yes, please. I'm looking for _____.

A: How about this(these)? This(These) _____ is(are) on sale today.

B: I like that(those) _____. Is that(Are those) on sale, too?

A: Yes, it's(they're) half price / it's(they're) a steal.

Unit 3 29

Out to the world with Mr. Moon!

A Vocabulary

Check the definitions of the following words and expressions again.

belt	blouse	boots	coat	dress	earrings	glasses	gloves
hat	half price	jacket	jeans	on sale	pajamas	pants	purse
shirt	shoes	skirt	socks	steal	sweater	tie	wear

B Reading

Read the story and mark each statement true [T] or false [F].

Brad is looking for a birthday present for his wife. He's at a store named Stacey's in the shopping mall. He's looking for nice earrings for her but all the earrings at the store are very expensive. He doesn't have much money so he's looking around here and there. There are some earrings on sale at another store named Mollie's. They're selling beautiful earrings at half price. He really likes them.

_____ 1. Brad is married.

_____ 2. He's looking for a birthday present for his sister.

_____ 3. He wants a nice necklace.

_____ 4. He has a lot of money now.

_____ 5. All the earrings are not expensive at Stacey's.

_____ 6. Mollie's is having a sale on earrings.

 **Writing**

Answer the questions.

1. Do you wear glasses?

2. What are you wearing today? Write down all the clothes you're wearing.

3. You need jeans. What would you say to a salesperson at a store?

4. You're a salesperson at a store. A customer is looking around. What would you say?

5. You want to ask if a shirt near you is on sale. What would you say?

6. You want to ask if a shirt far from you is on sale. What would you say?

Unit 4

Do You Have a Brother?

LESSON PLAN

1) Topic
- Family Members

2) Function
- Giving Information about Your Family
- Talking about Age

3) Grammar
- Have/Has
- Cardinal Numbers

Unit 4 Do you have a brother?

1 WORDS

1. son
2. daughter
3. mother
4. father
5. children
6. parents
7. grandmother
8. grandfather
9. granddaughter
10. grandson
11. grandchildren
12. sister
13. brother
14. uncle
15. aunt
16. cousin
17. nephew
18. niece
— me

2 GRAMMAR

Have/Has						
Affirmative		Questions		Short Answers		
I You We They	have a brother.	Do	I you we they	have a brother?	Yes,	I do. you do. we do. they do. he does. she does.	No,	I don't. you don't. we don't. they don't. he doesn't. she doesn't.
He She	has a brother.	Does	he she					

Cardinal Numbers				
16 sixteen	17 seventeen	18 eighteen	19 nineteen	20 twenty
21 twenty-one	22 twenty-two	30 thirty	40 forty	50 fifty
60 sixty	70 seventy	80 eighty	90 ninety	100 one hundred

A Circle the correct words.

1. She (have, has) a brother.
2. (Do, Does) he (have, has) a sister?
3. Bob doesn't (have, has) an uncle.
4. They (have, has) two sisters.
5. (Do, Does) you (have, has) any cousins?

B Rewrite the numbers into words like the example.

> She's **25** years old. ➡ She's **twenty-five** years old.

1. I have a big family of **40**. ➡ _____
2. My grandmother is **100** years old. ➡ _____
3. Jim has **15** cousins. ➡ _____
4. **65** children are having dinner together. ➡ _____
5. They have a **35**-year-old daughter. ➡ _____

C Practice conversations using the words below.

A: Who is she?
B: She's my sister.
A: What's her name?
B: Her name is Amanda.
A: How old is she?
B: She's eighteen years old.

my brothers
Paul (twenty),
Sam (twenty-two)

A: Who _____?
B: _____ my brothers.
A: _____ names?
B: _____ Paul and Sam.
A: How old _____?
B: Paul _____ years old and
Sam _____ years old.

my son
Peter (nineteen)

A: Who _____?
B: _____ my son.
A: _____ name?
B: _____ Peter.
A: How old _____?
B: _____ years old.

D Ask your partner if he(she) has any brothers or sisters using the questions below.

Do you have any sisters or brothers?
How many brothers(sisters) do you have?
What are their names?
How old are they?
What do they do?

Unit 4 35

3 CONVERSATION

A Listen and practice. 🎧 07

A: Do you have a brother?
B: Yes, I do. I have one brother.
A: What's his name?
B: His name is Warrick.
A: How old is he?
B: He's twenty-one years old.

B Work with a partner. Take turns to answer the questions.

A: Do you have a brother?

B: Yes, I do. I have one brother. / No, I don't.

1 he / nephews

A: _____?

B: No, _____.

2 they / nieces / three

A: _____?

B: Yes, _____. _____.

3 she / a cousin

A: _____?

B: No, _____.

4 your parents / brothers / four

A: _____?

B: Yes, _____. _____.

5 Sophie / children / two

A: _____?

B: Yes, _____. _____.

36 English Fly High | Check in

C Work with a partner. Take turns to ask and answer using the model conversation.

① A: Who is he?
B: He's **my brother**.
A: How old is he?
B: He's **twenty-one** years old.

② A: Who are they?
B: They're **my brothers**.
A: How old are they?
B: They're in their **thirties**.

twenties, thirties, forties, fifties, sixties, seventies, eighties

① my uncles / forties

② my mother / fifty-one

③ my aunts / twenties

④ my grandparents / sixties

⑤ my nephew / eighteen

D Do you have a family photo now? Tell your classmate about your family.
(Their names, ages, jobs, hobbies, etc.)

We are a family of four. (= My family has four members. / I have a family of four.)

Father, mother, one brother, and me.

This is my father. He's 56 years old. He's a high school teacher. His hobby is fishing…

Unit 4 37

Out to the world with Mr. Moon!

A Vocabulary

Check the definitions of the following words and expressions again.

father	mother	husband	wife	parents	children
son	daughter	brother	sister	grandfather	grandmother
grandchildren	grandson	granddaughter	uncle	aunt	niece
nephew	cousin	both			

B Reading

Read the story and circle the correct words.

I'm James. I have a big family. I live with my grandparents, father, mother, one brother, and one sister. My brother is Jack and my sister is Jackie. She lives with her husband Paul. They have a two-year-old son. His name is Fred. My father has two brothers. They're both in their forties. One is Jessie and the other is Joe. Jessie's not married. Joe's wife is Maggie. They have two daughters. Their names are Jennifer and Julie. Today is my grandfather's birthday. All my family members are here.

1. James has a (big, small) family.
2. James has (one, no) brother.
3. Fred is James' (niece, nephew).
4. His father has two (brothers, uncles).
5. Joe is James' (cousin, uncle).
6. Maggie is James' (sister, aunt).
7. Julie is James' (cousin, aunt).

C Writing

Look at the family tree below. Draw your own family tree and write down their names and relation to you.

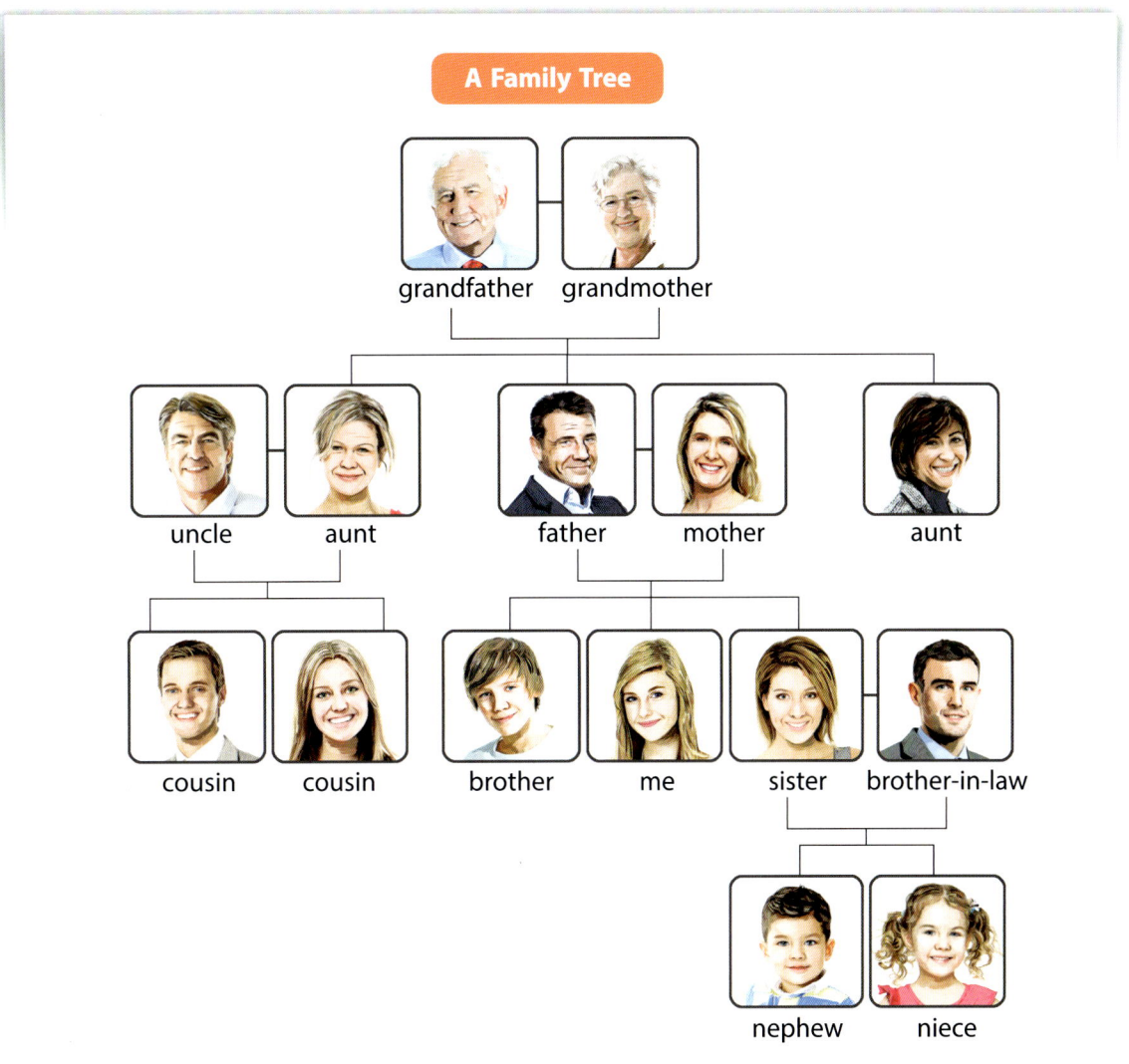

Unit 5

I Go Bungee Jumping on Saturdays.

LESSON PLAN

1. Topic
- Days and Months

2. Function
- Talking about Days, Dates, and Months
- Habitual Actions

3. Grammar
- It (pronoun)
- What + Noun + Be + It?
- Prepositions of Time (on, in, at)
- Ordinal Numbers

Unit 5 — I go bungee jumping on Saturdays.

1 WORDS

1. Sunday
2. Monday
3. Tuesday
4. Wednesday
5. Thursday
6. Friday
7. Saturday
8. January
9. February
10. March
11. April
12. May
13. June
14. July
15. August
16. September
17. October
18. November
19. December

Ordinal Numbers

1st	first	9th	ninth	17th	seventeenth
2nd	second	10th	tenth	18th	eighteenth
3rd	third	11th	eleventh	19th	nineteenth
4th	fourth	12th	twelfth	20th	twentieth
5th	fifth	13th	thirteenth	21st	twenty-first
6th	sixth	14th	fourteenth	22nd	twenty-second
7th	seventh	15th	fifteenth	23rd	twenty-third
8th	eighth	16th	sixteenth	30th	thirtieth

2 GRAMMAR

What + Noun + Be + It? / on, in, at (prepositions of time)			
Questions		Answers	
What	day is it? month is it? year is it? time is it? date is it?	It's	Sunday. September. 2015. 6 o'clock. September 1st (the first of September).

Prepositions of Time

on + day / date: on Sunday / on September 1st
at + time: at 6 o'clock
in + month / year: in September / in 2015

A Make questions using *what*.

1. A: _____
   B: It's 8 o'clock.

2. A: _____
   B: It's October.

3. A: _____
   B: It's April 22nd.

4. A: _____
   B: It's 2015.

5. A: _____
   B: It's Wednesday.

B Fill in the blanks using *at*, *on*, or *in*.

1. I go to school _____ 8 o'clock in the morning.
2. She does yoga _____ Fridays.
3. My mother was born _____ April 5th, 1941.
4. His birthday is _____ May.
5. The new department store opens _____ November 3rd.
6. Let's meet again _____ night.
7. I was born _____ 1995.

C Work with a partner. Take turns to ask and answer like the conversations below.

A: Do you go to church on Sundays?
B: No, I don't.
A: What do you do on Sundays?
B: I go shopping.

A: Does he swim on Saturdays?
B: No, he doesn't.
A: What does he do on Saturdays?
B: He goes fishing.

1. Mary / exercise / Mondays / go singing
2. you / clean your room / Fridays / go dancing
3. Mike / wash his car / Tuesdays / go bungee jumping
4. your parents / play tennis / Wednesdays / go hiking
5. Tom / study / Thursdays / go camping

D Work with a partner. Ask about days, dates, years, or birthdays.

What day is it today?

What date is it today?

What year is it?

What time is it?

When's your birthday?

Unit 5 43

3 CONVERSATION

A Listen and practice. 🎧 09

A: What do you do on weekdays?
B: I go to work.
A: Do you work on weekends?
B: No, I don't.
A: What do you do on Sundays?
B: I spend time with my family on Sundays.
A: Oh, good.

B Work with a partner. Practice the conversation above using the words below.

A: What do you do on weekdays?
B: I <u>work</u>.
A: What do you do on Sundays?
B: I <u>go to church</u>.

work / surf the Internet

A: What _____ Mandy do on weekdays?
B: _____.
A: What _____ do on Sundays?
B: _____.

go to school / go to the movies

A: What _____ Jeff and Kathy do on weekdays?
B: _____.
A: What _____ do on Sundays?
B: _____.

go to work / do yoga

A: What _____ you and your sister do on weekdays?
B: _____.
A: What _____ do on Sundays?
B: _____.

study / have a drink

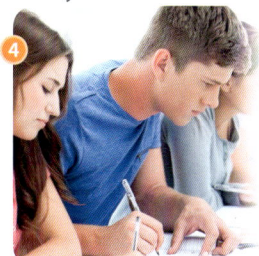

A: What _____ your friends do on weekdays?
B: _____.
A: What _____ do on Sundays?
B: _____.

baby-sit / sleep all day long

A: What _____ George do on weekdays?
B: _____.
A: What _____ do on Sundays?
B: _____.

C Work with a partner. Have a conversation using the sentences below.

A: What do you do in your free time?

B: I **go camping**. How about you?

A: I **go fishing**.

B: Cool.

1. go hiking / go shopping
2. go singing / go dancing
3. go mountain climbing / go bungee jumping
4. go walking / go jogging
5. go swimming / go scuba diving

D Now tell your partner or classmates about what you do on weekdays and weekends.

What do you do on weekdays?

What do you do on weekends?

What does your family do on Sundays?

What do your friends do on Sundays?

What do you do in your free time?

Out to the world with Mr. Moon!

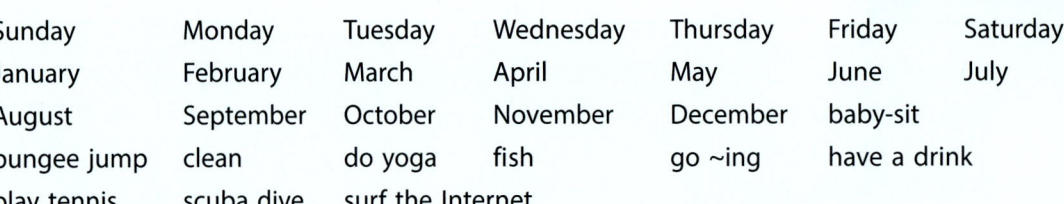

A Vocabulary

Check the definitions of the following words and expressions again.

Sunday	Monday	Tuesday	Wednesday	Thursday	Friday	Saturday
January	February	March	April	May	June	July
August	September	October	November	December	baby-sit	
bungee jump	clean	do yoga	fish	go ~ing	have a drink	
play tennis	scuba dive	surf the Internet				

B Reading

Read the story and choose the correct words.

Vivian works for the bank. She's very busy from Monday to Friday but she doesn't work on weekends.

She spends time with her family or friends in her free time. It's Saturday today. On Saturday mornings she goes swimming because the swimming teacher is handsome. On Saturday evenings she goes shopping or sees a movie with her friends. On Sunday mornings she goes to church with her family. On Sunday afternoons she has a big lunch with them. On Sunday evenings she surfs the Internet, watches TV, or takes a walk with her dog. She really loves her free time.

1. Vivian works for _____.
   a. the bank   b. a company
2. She doesn't work on _____.
   a. Friday   b. Saturday
3. On Saturday mornings she goes _____.
   a. swimming   b. shopping
4. On Saturday evenings she sees a movie with her _____.
   a. family   b. friends

5. On Sunday mornings she goes to _____.
   a. church   b. the swimming pool
6. On Sunday afternoons she has a big _____.
   a. date   b. lunch
7. On Sunday evenings she surfs _____.
   a. in the sea   b. the Internet

C Writing

Write down the answers to the questions.

1. What's the date today?

2. What day is it?

3. What time is it?

4. What do you do on weekdays?

5. What do you do on weekends?

6. What do you do in your free time?

7. Make a weekly schedule.

Sunday	Monday	Tuesday

Wednesday	Thursday	Friday	Saturday

Unit 6

My Favorite Sport Is Soccer.

LESSON PLAN

1. Topic
- Hobbies and Tastes

2. Function
- Talking about What You Enjoy
- Asking and Answering about Your Favorite Things

3. Grammar
- Like + Noun
- What kind of + Noun + do you like?
- What is your favorite + Noun?

Unit 6 My favorite sport is soccer.

1 WORDS

  classical music / pop music

music

  baseball / basketball

sports

  rock music / jazz

   football / soccer / golf

2 GRAMMAR

Like + Noun	
Statements	**Questions**
I / you / we / they like soccer.	Do I / you / we / they like soccer?
He / She / It likes soccer.	Does he / she / it like soccer?
Answers	
Yes, I / you / we / they do.	No, I / you / we / they don't.
Yes, he / she / it does.	No, he / she / it doesn't.

What kind(s) of + noun + do you like?: What kinds of sports do you like?
　　　　　　　　　　　　　　　　　What kind of music do you like?
What is your favorite + noun?: What is your favorite sport?

A Fill in the blanks using *like*.

1. I _____ music.
2. Does she _____ movies?
3. Dave _____ soccer.
4. Do you and your brother _____ baseball?
5. What do Willy and his friends _____ ?
6. Tell me what Carl really _____ .

B Fill in the blanks like the model conversation below.

A: What kinds of movies do you like?
B: I like horror movies.

1. **sports / he / baseball**

   A: What kinds of _____ like?
   B: _____.

2. **flowers / Carol and Josh / roses**

   A: What kinds of _____ like?
   B: _____.

3. **books / Marilyn / comic books**

   A: What kinds of _____ like?
   B: _____.

4. **movies / you / science fiction movies**

   A: What kinds of _____ like?
   B: _____.

C Work with a partner. Take turns to ask and answer like the conversations below.

A: <u>What</u>'s your favorite <u>color</u>?
B: My favorite <u>color</u> is <u>purple</u>.

1. Who / actor / Tom Cruise
2. What / book / the Harry Potter series
3. What / sport / basketball

A: <u>Who</u>'s your favorite <u>singer</u>?
B: My favorite <u>singer</u> is <u>Taylor Swift</u>.

4. Who / soccer player / Beckham
5. What / drama / the Big Bang Theory
6. What / movie / Forrest Gump

D Work with a partner. Take turns to ask and answer like below.

A: Do you like ~? (dogs, cats, rain, apples, snakes, English...)
B: Yes, I love ~. / No, I don't. I like ~.

Unit 6 51

3 CONVERSATION

A Listen and practice.

A: What kinds of sports do you like?

B: I like baseball. What's your favorite sport?

A: My favorite sport is soccer.

　Do you like soccer?

B: Yes, but I just watch it on TV.

A: Who's your favorite soccer player?

B: My favorite soccer player is Messi.

B Work with a partner. Take turns to make the questions.

A: What kinds of **sports** do you like?

B: What's your favorite **sport**?

❶ A: What kinds of movies do you like?

　B: _____

❷ A: What kinds of books do you like?

　B: _____

❸ A: What kinds of animals do you like?

　B: _____

❹ A: What kind of music do you like?

　B: _____

❺ A: What kind of food do you like?

　B: _____

C Work with a partner. Take turns to ask and answer using the model conversation.

A: Do you like **animals**?
B: Of course. I love **animals**. How about you?
A: Me, too. My favorite **animal** is **a cat**.

1. books, Hamlet
    A: Do you like _____?
    B: Of course. I love _____. How about you?
    A: Me, too. My favorite _____ is _____.

2. sports, football
    A: Do you like _____?
    B: Of course. I love _____. How about you?
    A: Me, too. My favorite _____ is _____.

3. fruits, an orange
    A: Do you like _____?
    B: Of course. I love _____. How about you?
    A: Me, too. My favorite _____ is _____.

4. music, rock music
    A: Do you like _____?
    B: Of course. I love _____. How about you?
    A: Me, too. My favorite _____ is _____.

5. movies, About Time
    A: Do you like _____?
    B: Of course. I love _____. How about you?
    A: Me, too. My favorite _____ is _____.

D Work with a partner. Ask him(her) what he(she) likes.

What kind of music do you like?
Who's your favorite singer or player?
What kinds of books do you like?
What's your favorite food?
Who's your favorite actor?
What kinds of sports do you like?

Out to the world with Mr. Moon!

A Vocabulary

Check the definitions of the following words and expressions again.

romantic comedy	western	science fiction movie		
horror movie	comic book	novel	poetry	biography
classical music	popular music	jazz	rock music	baseball
basketball	football	golf	soccer	volleyball
favorite	kind	player	snake	

B Reading

Read the story and answer the questions.

I'm Lily. I like animals. My favorite animal is a dog. I have a puppy. Its name is Pinky. Pink is my favorite color. Pinky is very cute and energetic. I walk it every morning. My sister Joan likes her yellow sweater. It's nice and warm. Yellow is her favorite color. I like her sweater, but she doesn't let me wear it.

My brother Billy likes music. He is a big fan of rock music. His favorite band is Radiohead. He has a T-shirt. It has a picture of the band. The T-shirt is his favorite thing. He always wears it.

1. Does Lily like animals?
2. What's her favorite animal?
3. Does Lily walk her puppy every night?
4. What is Lily's favorite color?
5. Is Joan's favorite color pink?
6. Does Lily sometimes wear her sister's sweater?
7. Does Billy like classical music?
8. What's his favorite thing?

C Writing

Write down your favorite thing.

favorite food: **My favorite food is** _____

1. favorite movie: _____

2. favorite sport: _____

3. favorite music: _____

4. favorite actor or actress: _____

5. favorite clothes: _____

6. favorite animal: _____

Unit 7

I Usually Drink Coffee Five Times a Day.

LESSON PLAN

1 Topic
- Frequencies

2 Function
- Describing the Frequency of Actions

3 Grammar
- Frequency Adverbs
- Subject + Be + Frequency Adverbs
- The Number of Times

Unit 7 I usually drink coffee five times a day.

1 WORDS

Frequency Adverb

1. always
2. usually
3. often
4. sometimes
5. rarely
6. never

2 GRAMMAR

Frequency Adverbs	
Questions	Answers (Subject + Frequency Adverb + Verb)
How often do I drink coffee?	You always drink coffee.
How often do you drink coffee?	I usually drink coffee.
How often does he drink coffee?	He often drinks coffee.
How often does she drink coffee?	She sometimes drinks coffee.
How often do we drink coffee?	We rarely drink coffee.
How often do they drink coffee?	They never drink coffee.

Subject + Be + Frequency Adverb

: Coffee is always (usually, often, sometimes, rarely, never) good for you.

The Number of Times

: I drink coffee once (twice, three times, four times, five times…) a day.

A Add the frequency adverbs to the sentences.

> I get up at six o'clock. (always) ➔ I always get up at six o'clock.

1. Sheena goes swimming on Fridays. (usually) ➔ _____
2. My parents help me with my homework. (sometimes) ➔ _____
3. David eats chocolate. (never) ➔ _____
4. Do you go to the movies? (often) ➔ _____
5. Kelly eats lettuce. (rarely) ➔ _____

B Put the words in the correct order.

sad / never / my / sister / is → My sister is never sad.

1. is / sometimes / Morris / angry → _____
2. are / We / often / tired → _____
3. good for you / is / Too much caffeine / rarely → _____
4. My neighbors / sometimes / noisy / are → _____
5. Cats / are / friendly / rarely → _____
6. usually / good at English / is / Matt → _____

C Work with a partner. Take turns to ask and answer like the conversation below.

A: Do you usually get up early?
B: No, I <u>rarely</u> get up early. I <u>usually</u> get up <u>late</u>.

① A: Do you usually go to work by bus?
   B: rarely / by subway

② A: Does Lynn usually exercise in the morning?
   B: sometimes / in the evening

③ A: Does your family usually eat out on Saturdays?
   B: rarely / on Sundays

④ A: Does Charlie usually drink coffee at night?
   B: never / in the morning

⑤ A: Does your husband usually read the newspaper in the bathroom?
   B: sometimes / in the living room

⑥ A: Is Mrs. Williams usually quiet?
   B: never / talkative

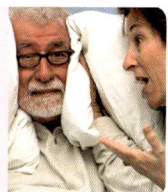

D Work with a partner. Take turns to answer these questions. There are lots of possible answers. And why don't you make questions on your own?

A: What animal usually has red eyes?
B: A rabbit usually has red eyes.

1. What animal rarely moves fast?
2. What animal always has a long neck?
3. What animal usually jumps in Australia?
4. What animal always eats bamboo in China?
5. What bird never flies?

3 CONVERSATION

A Listen and practice.

A: How often do you drink coffee?
B: I usually drink coffee five times a day.
A: Five times a day? Well, you drink too much.
B: I'm healthy and I always sleep well.
A: I rarely drink coffee. Too much coffee is rarely good for you.
B: I often eat fresh fruits and vegetables.

B Work with a partner. Practice conversations like below.

A: How often **do you drink coffee**?
B: **I drink coffee five times a day.**

A: How often **is your daughter kind to you?**
B: **She is kind to me twice a month.**

1. your husband, have a drink, twice a week

   A: How often _____?
   B: _____

2. Alan, is late for school, every day

   A: How often _____?
   B: _____

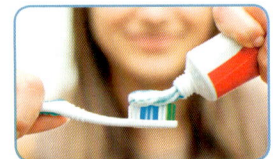

3. you, brush your teeth, three times a day

   A: How often _____?
   B: _____

4. they, go to the gym, four times a week

   A: How often _____?
   B: _____

5. your brother, clean his room, once a year

   A: How often _____?
   B: _____

C Work with a partner. Take turns to ask and answer using the model conversation.

> A: I usually **drink coffee five times a day**.
> B: **Five times a day? Well, you drink too much.**
>   **I rarely drink coffee.**

1. **eat fried chicken / four times a week**
   A: I usually _____.
   B: _____
      _____

2. **read books / 10 hours a day**
   A: I usually _____.
   B: _____
      _____

3. **have soda / five times a day**
   A: I usually _____.
   B: _____
      _____

4. **spend time at work / 12 hours a day**
   A: I usually _____.
   B: _____
      _____

5. **have meat / seven times a week**
   A: I usually _____.
   B: _____
      _____

D Work with a partner. Ask him(her) how often he(she) does something.

How often do you exercise?
How often do you go hiking?
How often do you wash your hair?
How often do you go to the movies?
How often do you travel?
How often do you have bad dreams?

Out to the world with Mr. Moon!

A Vocabulary

Check the definitions of the following words and expressions again.

always	usually	often	sometimes	rarely	never
eat out	friendly	fruit	give up	kind	part-time job
talkative	vegetable				

B Reading

Read the story and circle the correct words.

Chuck is my brother. He rarely gets up early in the morning. He usually doesn't eat breakfast because he doesn't have time for breakfast. He always goes to school by subway. He is sometimes late for school. He is usually sleepy all day long so he drinks coffee five times a day. He has a part-time job so he usually goes to work after school. He works five times a week. He sometimes sees his friends in his free time. He usually comes back home at 10 o'cloc and he does his homework until late at night. He is often tired but he is never sad. I'm always proud of him.

1. Chuck (usually, rarely) gets up early.
2. He usually (eats, doesn't eat) breakfast.
3. He always goes to school by (subway, bus).
4. He is (sometimes, rarely) late for school.
5. He usually (sees his friends, goes to work) after school.
6. He works (five times, three times) a week.
7. He is (always, often) tired.
8. He is never (unhappy, happy).

C Writing

What do you do every day? Write down your everyday routines using frequency adverbs (always, usually, often, sometimes, rarely, never).

→ I usually get up at 5 o'clock in the morning.
I always jog in the morning.

Unit 8

It's Raining a Lot Today.

LESSON PLAN

1. Topic
- Weather
- Likes and Dislikes

2. Function
- Describing Weather in Various Cities
- Taking about What You Want to Do

3. Grammar
- Want to + Base verb
- It (Pronoun: Impersonal Subject) + Adjectives about Weather

Unit 8 It's raining a lot today.

1 WORDS

1. sunny
2. cloudy
3. rainy (raining)
4. windy
5. snowy (snowing)
6. hot
7. warm
8. cool
9. cold
10. spring
11. summer
12. fall (= autumn)
13. winter

2 GRAMMAR

Want to + Base verb / It (Pronoun: Impersonal Subject)	
Statements	Questions
I / You / We / They want to play tennis. He / She wants to play tennis.	Do I / you / we / they want to play tennis? Does he / she want to play tennis?
Questions	Answers
What's the weather like?	It's sunny / cloudy / rainy / windy / snowy.
How's the weather?	It's hot / warm / cool / cold.
What's the temperature?	It's 20℃ (= twenty degrees Celsius). It's 50°F (= fifty degrees Fahrenheit).
What season is it?	It's spring / summer / fall / winter.

A Match the answers.

1. What's the weather like today?
2. What's the temperature now?
3. How's the weather in summer?
4. What season is it these days?
5. Is it still cold outside?

a. It's hot and humid in summer.
b. No, it's warm.
c. It's cloudy.
d. It's 23℃.
e. It's spring.

B Rewrite these sentences.

> I want some spaghetti. (have) ➡ I want to have some spaghetti.

1. I want this bag. (have) ➡ _____
2. Angela wants a vacation. (take) ➡ _____
3. Do you want those blue jeans? (wear) ➡ _____
4. We want some milk. (drink) ➡ _____

C Work with a partner. Take turns to ask and answer like the conversation below.

> A: What's the weather like in **Seoul**?
> B: **It's hot.** How's the weather in **New York**?
> A: **It's cool.**

1. Tokyo – cold / Sydney – warm

   A: What's the weather like in _____?
   B: _____. How's the weather in _____?
   A: _____.

2. Hong Kong – raining / Toronto – snowing

   A: What's the weather like in _____?
   B: _____. How's the weather in _____?
   A: _____.

3. London – foggy / Shanghai – windy

   A: What's the weather like in _____?
   B: _____. How's the weather in _____?
   A: _____.

4. Boston – freezing / Athens – humid

   A: What's the weather like in _____?
   B: _____. How's the weather in _____?
   A: _____.

5. Paris – cool / Berlin – chilly

   A: What's the weather like in _____?
   B: _____. How's the weather in _____?
   A: _____.

D Work with a partner. Talk about today's weather.

1. What's the weather like today?
2. What's the temperature now?
3. How's the weather in spring?
4. What season is it these days?
5. What's your favorite season?
6. Why do you like spring / summer / fall / winter?
7. Do you like rain?

3 CONVERSATION

A Listen and practice. 🎧 15

A: How's the weather today?
B: It's raining a lot.
A: What's the temperature now?
B: It's 26℃. It's still hot.
A: I hate rain. I want to go outside.
B: Me, too. Do you want to play table tennis?
A: Sounds great.

B Work with a partner. Practice the conversation like below.

cool / hot
A: How's the weather today? Is it **cool**?
B: No, it's still **hot**.
A: I hate **hot** weather.

warm / cold
A: How's the weather today? Is it _____?
B: No, it's still _____.
A: I hate _____ weather.

sunny / rainy
A: How's the weather today? Is it _____?
B: No, it's still _____.
A: I hate _____ weather.

dry / humid
A: How's the weather today? Is it _____?
B: No, it's still _____.
A: I hate _____ weather.

warm / chilly
A: How's the weather today? Is it _____?
B: No, it's still _____.
A: I hate _____ weather.

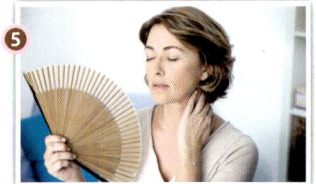

cool / steamy
A: How's the weather today? Is it _____?
B: No, it's still _____.
A: I hate _____ weather.

C Work with a partner. Take turns to ask and answer using the model conversation.

> A: I want to go outside.
> B: Me, too. Do you want to **play table tennis**?
> A: **Sounds great**.

1. take a walk / That's a great idea.

2. go bowling / Sounds nice.

3. play badminton / Sounds good.

4. go skateboarding / Excellent.

5. play basketball / Sounds awesome.

D Work with a partner. Take turns to ask and answer questions like below. And make your own questions.

What do you like to do on sunny / rainy / snowy days?

What do you like to eat on rainy days or hot summer days?

Do you put on rainwear or rain boots?

What color of rain boots do you want to have?

What do you want to do on the first snowy day of this year?

Who do you want to see on the first snowy day of this year?

Out to the world with Mr. Moon!

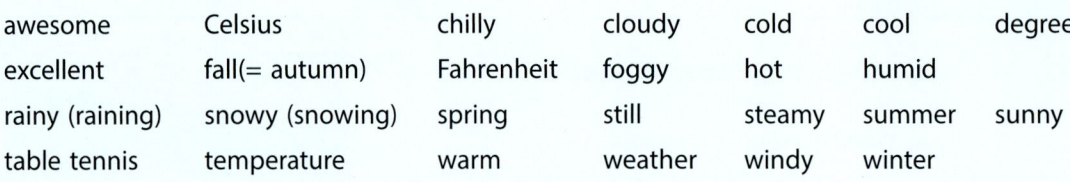

A Vocabulary

Check the definitions of the following words and expressions again.

awesome	Celsius	chilly	cloudy	cold	cool	degree
excellent	fall(= autumn)	Fahrenheit	foggy	hot	humid	
rainy (raining)	snowy (snowing)	spring	still	steamy	summer	sunny
table tennis	temperature	warm	weather	windy	winter	

B Reading

Read the story and mark each statement true [T] or false [F].

It rained all day long today. It's still raining now. School is over. I want to go home but I don't have an umbrella. I'm walking in the rain so I'm very wet. I want to take off my wet clothes and take a hot shower because I don't want to catch a cold. I want to have something hot. I always want to have hot chocolate and pancake on rainy days. Actually I don't like rainy days and I hate summer. My favorite season is fall. It's cool. We have clear blue skies and colorful leaves. Everything is so beautiful in fall. I want to say good bye to summer and say hello to fall.

_____ 1. It's cloudy.

_____ 2. He's at school now.

_____ 3. He's doesn't have an umbrella.

_____ 4. He wants to have hot chocolate.

_____ 5. He likes summer.

_____ 6. His favorite season is summer.

_____ 7. We have colorful leaves in winter.

_____ 8. He's looking forward to autumn.

C Writing

Write down the weather during the last 7 days using the words below.

| sunny | cloudy | rainy | windy | snowy | chilly | cold |
| cool | freezing | humid | hot | steamy | warm | |

Day	Sunday	Monday	Tuesday	Wednesday	Thursday	Friday	Saturday
Date							
Weather							
Temperature							

Unit 9

Can You Ride a Bicycle?

LESSON PLAN

1. **Topic**
   - Talents and Abilities

2. **Function**
   - Expressing People's Talents and Abilities

3. **Grammar**
   - Can (Ability) + Base verb
   - Be Good at + Noun / ~ing

Unit 9 Can you ride a bicycle?

1 WORDS

1. cook
2. dance
3. drive a car
4. fix a car
5. paint
6. ride a bicycle
7. play the piano
8. sing
9. skate
10. ski

2 GRAMMAR

Can (Ability) + Base verb				
Statements		**Questions**		
I You He/She We They	can ride a bicycle.	Can	I you he/she we they	ride a bicycle?
Answers				
Yes,	you can. I can. he/she can. we can. they can.	No,		you can't. I can't. he/she can't. we can't. they can't.

> be good at + noun
> I'm good at mathematics.

> be good at + ~ing(base verb+ing)
> I'm good at riding a bicycle.

A Fill in the blanks.

> Can birds fly? Yes, **they can fly**.

1. Can you in-line skate?   No, _____.
2. Can she sing a song?   Yes, _____.
3. Can he stand on his head?   Yes, _____.
4. Can Jack solve the problem?   No, _____.
5. Can your sister drive a car?   Yes, _____.

B Work with a partner. Practice the conversation like below.

A: Can **you play the piano**?

B: No, **I can't** but **I can play the guitar**.

1. Jane / speak English / French
   A: Can _____?
   B: No, _____
      but _____.

2. you / ride a motorcycle / bicycle
   A: Can _____?
   B: No, _____
      but _____.

3. they / play baseball / basketball
   A: Can _____?
   B: No, _____
      but _____.

4. Bill / ski / skate
   A: Can _____?
   B: No, _____
      but _____.

5. Mr. Moor / read Chinese characters / the Korean alphabet
   A: Can _____?
   B: No, _____
      but _____.

C Work with a partner. Take turns to ask and answer.

A: Can you cook Korean food?

B: Sure. **I'm good at cooking Korean food.**

1. A: Can your parents speak Japanese?
   B: Sure. _____.

2. A: Can Fred play tennis?
   B: Sure. _____.

3. A: Can Roger paint pictures?
   B: Sure. _____.

4. A: Can Betty bake apple pies?
   B: Sure. _____.

5. A: Can your friends dance?
   B: Sure. _____.

D Work with a partner. Take turns to ask and answer about what he(she) can and can't do like below.

A: Can you ride a horse?

B: Sure, I'm good at riding horses. / No, I can't but I can in-line skate.

Unit **9** 75

3 CONVERSATION

A Listen and practice.

A: Wow! You can in-line skate very well.
B: Thanks. Can you, too?
A: Not so well. Can you ride a bicycle?
B: I am pretty good at riding a bicycle. What about you?
A: I can even ride it with one hand.
B: Really? Let's go bike riding.

B Work with a partner. Practice conversations like below.

A: Wow! You can **paint pictures** very well.
B: Thanks. Can you **paint pictures**, too?
A: No, I can't **paint them**.

play the drums

A: Wow! You can _____ very well.
B: Thanks. Can you _____, too?
A: No, I can't _____.

bake cakes

A: Wow! You can _____ very well.
B: Thanks. Can you _____, too?
A: No, I can't _____.

ride a horse

A: Wow! You can _____ very well.
B: Thanks. Can you _____, too?
A: No, I can't _____.

make sandwiches

A: Wow! You can _____ very well.
B: Thanks. Can you _____, too?
A: No, I can't _____.

fix a car

A: Wow! You can _____ very well.
B: Thanks. Can you _____, too?
A: No, I can't _____.

C Work with a partner. Take turns to ask and answer using the model conversation.

A: Can you ride a bicycle?

B: Of course. I am pretty good at riding bicycles.

1. Jack / fix radios
2. you / cut hair
3. Josh and Bruce / play table tennis
4. Lindsay / paint houses
5. Brian / speak Chinese

D Work with a partner.

→ Write five true sentences about things you can and can't do. Then write five false sentences about things you can and can't do.

True	False
I can play the piano.	I can play the guitar.
I can't ski.	I can't skate.

→ Take turns to read your sentences to your partner. Ask him(or her) to guess whether you're telling the truth or not like below.

A: I can play the guitar.
B: False.
A: Yes, that's false. I can't play the guitar.

Out to the world with Mr. Moon!

A Vocabulary

Check the definitions of the following words and expressions again.

athletic	bake	be good at	Chinese characters	cook
dance	drive a car	fix a car	paint	ride a bicycle
play the piano	physical education teacher		sing	skate
ski	various			

B Reading

Read the story and answer the questions.

Judy is looking for a job. She can act, sing, dance, and she's pretty good at playing various musical instruments. She can play the piano, the guitar, and the drums. She wants to be a musical singer. She's preparing for an audition so she does her exercises and practices every day. She has a sister. Her name is Holly. She is looking for a job, too. She's good at all sports. She can play basketball, volleyball, and even soccer. She can swim very well. She's very athletic. She wants to be a physical education teacher.

1. What are they looking for?

2. What can Judy do?

3. What musical instruments can Judy play?

4. What does Judy want to be?

5. Does Judy have a sister?

6. Is Holly good at all kinds of music?

7. Can Holly swim?

8. What does Holly want to be?

C Writing

Suppose you're looking for a job. So you're having an interview now. Answer the questions and write down your skills.

A: What's your name?

B: _____

A: What kind of job are you looking for?

B: _____

A: Tell me about your skills. What can you do?

B: I can _____

Unit 10

Can I Have French fries?

LESSON PLAN

1) Topic
- Permission and Request

2) Function
- Expressing Permission and Request
- Expressing Obligation

3) Grammar
- Can (Permission) + Base verb
- Have to/Has to

Unit 10 — Can I have French fries?

1 WORDS

 1. answer the phone
 2. clean the room
 3. drive a car
 4. go to a party
 5. go to a soccer game
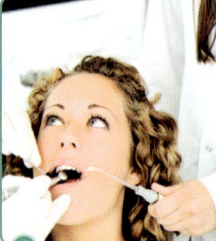 6. go to the dentist
 7. go to the movies
 8. make a sandwich
 9. see a doctor

2 GRAMMAR

Can (Permission / Request)			
	Questions	Polite Questions	Answers
Permission	Can I have French fries?	Could I have French fries?	Yes, you can. No, you can't.
Request	Can you help me?	Could you help me?	Yes, I can. No, I can't.

Have (Has) to + Base verb	
Statements	Questions
I / You / We / They have to go. He / She / It has to go.	Do I / you / we / they have to go? Does he / she / it have to go?

A Match the questions to the answer.

1. Can I go out?
2. Can I drink your coffee?
3. Can my friends come over here?
4. Can I drive your car?
5. Can we make sandwiches?
6. Can I use your phone?

a. No, you can't. You don't have a driver's license.
b. No, we can't. There isn't any bread.
c. No, you can't. It's out of batteries.
d. Yes, you can. It's tasty.
e. Yes, you can but you have to be back by 12 o'clock.
f. Yes, they can. I really want to see them.

B Circle the correct words.

1. Does Molly (have to, has to) leave now?

2. My brother (have to, has to) see a doctor.

3. Jim has to (washes, wash) his clothes.

4. What (do, does) he have to do today?

5. You have to (be, are) quiet in public places.

C Work with a partner. Take turns to ask and answer.

A: Can we go to the movies?
B: No, we can't. We have to go to Margaret's house.

1. A: Can I have little homework? (study hard)
   B: No, _____. _____

2. A: Can I stay up till midnight? (get up early)
   B: No, _____. _____

3. A: Can we eat turkey now? (wait for thirty minutes)
   B: No, _____. _____

4. A: Can I quit my job? (make money)
   B: No, _____. _____

5. A: Can I buy a new car? (save money)
   B: No, _____. _____

D Do you want to ask something to your teacher about your English lesson? Write down a very polite note about what you ask using "Could we~?".

Could we have our lesson outside?

Could we go to a karaoke after class?

Could we learn more grammar?

Could we have more homework?

3 CONVERSATION

A Listen and practice. 🎧 19

A: Can I have French fries?
B: No, you can't. They're not good for your health.
A: Can I have a hamburger?
B: No, you can't. You have to eat healthy food like fresh vegetables.
A: Then I have to eat chicken salad. Can you give me some salad?
B: Sure. Be my guest.

B Work with a partner. Practice the conversation using the words below.

A: Can **I have French fries**?
B: No, you can't. You have to **eat healthy food like fresh vegetables**.

1. **have a hamburger / eat a salad**

   A: Can I _____?

   B: No, you can't. You have to _____.

2. **go to the movies / take care of the babies**

   A: Can I _____?

   B: No, you can't. You have to _____.

3. **go to Henry's party / clean your room**

   A: Can I _____?

   B: No, you can't. You have to _____.

4. **have some cake / lose weight**

   A: Can I _____?

   B: No, you can't. You have to _____.

5. **go to a soccer game / go to the dentist**

   A: Can I _____?

   B: No, you can't. You have to _____.

C Work with a partner. Take turns to ask and answer using the model conversation.

A: Can you **give me some salad**?
B: **Sure. Be my guest.** / **I'm sorry but I can't.**

1. lend me some money / I'm sorry but I can't.
2. pass me the salt / Sure. Here you are.
3. give me a small plate / I'm sorry but I can't.
4. feed my dog / Sure. Be my guest.
5. answer the phone / I'm sorry but I can't.

D Work with a partner. Take turns to ask each other to do something and do it like below. And ask more.

A: Could you pass me my purse, please?
B: Sure. Here you are. (Pass your partner a purse.)

A: Could you open the door, please?
B: Sure. Be my guest. (Open the door.)

Out to the world with Mr. Moon!

A Vocabulary

Check the definitions of the following words and expressions again.

answer the phone	clean the room	drive a car	go to a party
go to a soccer game	go to the dentist	go to the movies	make a sandwich
pass ~ pepper	see a doctor		

B Reading

Read the story below and correct the wrong sentences.

Jessica is a mother of three children. She has to get up early because she has to do a lot of things in the morning. She has to make breakfast, wake her children up, help them get dressed and get them ready for school. Her children say, "Can you give me a drink?," "Can you pass me some bread?," "Can you cut my eggs?," and "Can you give me some money?" After breakfast, she has to drive them to school and then she goes to work. In the afternoon, her children come home. They say, "Can you help me with my homework?," "Can I play with my friends?," and "Can I go to a party?" In the evening, she has to clean her house and wash clothes. She is very busy every day. She loves her children but she is sometimes tired.

1. Jessica has three dogs. ➡ _____
2. She doesn't get up early in the morning. ➡ _____
3. She doesn't have to make breakfast. ➡ _____
4. Her children walk to school. ➡ _____
5. Her children can do their homework by themselves. ➡ _____
6. Her children come home in the evening. ➡ _____
7. She isn't so busy on weekdays. ➡ _____

C Writing

Suppose you're having dinner with someone at the restaurant. You need a lot of help from him. Ask him to do something for you using "Could you~?" and the words below.

| give | pass | me | the menu | a small plate |
| a drink | a knife | the pepper | the salt |

1. Could you _____?

2. Could you _____?

3. Could you _____?

4. Could you _____?

5. Could you _____?

6. Could you _____?

Answers

Answers

Unit 1 Is he good-looking?

❷ GRAMMAR

A
1. Is it / it isn't
2. Are they / they aren't
3. Is it / it isn't
4. Is he / he isn't
5. Is she / she isn't
6. Is she / she isn't

B
1. Is Bobby handsome or ugly?
2. Is Kate young or old?
3. Are they tall or short?
4. Is your hair curly or straight?
5. Is her house large or small?

C
1. he isn't   2. he is   3. it is
4. they aren't   5. it is

D
1. I'm single.   2. It's long.   3. It's stupid.
4. They're quiet.   5. She is shy.

❸ CONVERSATION

B
1. your boyfriend / Is he strong or weak / He's strong / Is he / he is
2. Henry / Is he thin or fat / He's fat / Is he / he is
3. Gloria / Is she smart or stupid / She's smart / Is she / she is
4. Mike / Is he married or single / He's single / Is he / he is
5. Rachel / Is she fair-skinned or dark-skinned / She's fair-skinned / Is she / she is

C
1. Are / I'm   2. Is / She is   3. Are / They are
4. Are / They are   5. Is / He is

Out to the world with Mr. Moon

A Vocabulary

young/new - old 젊은 / 새로운 – 늙은 / 오래된
married - single 결혼한 – 미혼의
beautiful/pretty - ugly 아름다운/예쁜 – 못생긴
noisy - quiet 시끄러운 – 조용한
curly - straight 곱슬곱슬한 – 직모의
strong - weak 힘이 센 – 약한
different 다른

heavy/fat - thin 무거운/살찐 – 마른
handsome - ugly 잘생긴 – 못생긴
large/big - small/little 큰 – 작은
rich - poor 부유한 – 가난한
fair-skinned - dark-skinned (피부가) 흰 – 거무스름한
active - shy 활동적인 – 수줍은
good-looking 외모가 준수한, 예쁜

B Reading

1. Sandy has a (sister, brother) called Sandra.
2. They look very (alike, different).
3. Sandy has (blue, brown) eyes.
4. Sandra's hair is (straight, curly).
5. Sandra is (tall and thin, short and heavy).
6. Sandy is (fair-skinned, dark-skinned).
7. Sandra is (shy, active).

Unit 2 What are you doing?

❷ GRAMMAR

A
1. We're reading a book.
2. She's drinking milk.
3. They're watching TV.
4. He's eating breakfast.
5. You're studying English.

B
1. What are we doing?
2. What is she doing?
3. What are they doing?
4. What is he doing?
5. What am I doing?

C
1. What is / He's reading
2. What are / We're watching
3. What is / She's cooking
4. What are / They're studying
5. What is / He's driving
6. What are / They're playing

❸ CONVERSATION

B
1. is Lisa / She's / kitchen / is she / She's cooking dinner
2. are you / I'm / living room / are you / I'm listening to music
3. are Henry and his friends / They're / yard / are they / They're playing basketball
4. is Susan / She's / dining room / is she / She's drinking milk
5. is Jane / She's / park / is she / She's talking on the phone
6. are you and Judy / We're / restaurant / are you / We're eating lunch

C
1. A: Is your cat sleeping?
   B: No, it isn't. It's eating fish now.
2. A: Is Karen studying?
   B: No, she isn't. She's taking a shower now.
3. A: Is Jim swimming?
   B: No, he isn't. He's playing the guitar now.
4. A: Are they working?
   B: No, they aren't. They're playing cards now.
5. A: Are the girls dancing?
   B: No, they aren't. They're singing now.

Out to the world with Mr. Moon

A Vocabulary

cooking 요리하고 있는	drinking 마시고 있는	driving 운전하고 있는	eating 먹고 있는	listening 듣고 있는
playing 놀고 (연주하고) 있는	reading 읽고 있는	singing 노래하고 있는	sleeping 자고 있는	studying 공부하고 있는
swimming 수영하고 있는	watching 지켜보고 있는	working 일하고 있는	talking on the phone 전화 통화하고 있는	

B Reading
1. They're at the beach.
2. It's nice.
3. He's reading a book.
4. Yes, they are.
5. He's playing the guitar.
6. No, he isn't.
7. She is eating a sandwich.
8. They're playing beach volleyball.

Unit 3 This shirt is on sale today.

2 GRAMMAR

A

[s]	[z]	[iz]
shirts	gloves	blouses
boots	earrings	dresses
jackets	jeans	glasses
pants	pajamas	purses
skirts	shoes	
socks	sweaters	

B
1. (This, These) is a nice blouse.
2. I like (that, those) gloves.
3. Is (this, these) sweater expensive?
4. (That, Those) are my jeans.
5. Are (this, these) your earrings?

C
1. these / These boots are / those / those boots
2. this / This hat is / that / that hat
3. these / These glasses are / those / those glasses
4. this / This coat is / that / that coat

3 CONVERSATION

B
1. pants / these / These pants are / those pants / Are those
2. a belt / this / This belt is / that belt / Is that
3. shoes / these / These shoes are / those shoes / Are those
4. a jacket / this / This jacket is / that jacket / Is that
5. socks / these / These socks are / those socks / Are those

Out to the world with Mr. Moon

A Vocabulary

belt 벨트 blouse 블라우스 boots 장화 coat 코트 dress 옷, 원피스
earrings 귀걸이 glasses 안경 gloves 장갑 hat 모자 half price 반값
jacket 상의 jeans 청바지 on sale 세일 중 pajamas 잠옷 pants 바지
purse 핸드백 shirt 셔츠 shoes 신발 skirt 치마 socks 양말
steal 공짜, 훔치다 sweater 스웨터 tie 넥타이 wear 입다

B Reading

 T 1. Brad is married.
 F 2. He's looking for a birthday present for his sister.
 F 3. He wants a nice necklace.
 F 4. He has a lot of money now.
 F 5. All the earrings are not expensive at Stacey's.
 T 6. Mollie's is having a sale on earrings.

Unit 4 Do you have a brother?

❷ GRAMMAR

A 1. She (have, **has**) a brother.
2. (Do, **Does**) he (**have**, has) a sister?
3. Bob doesn't (**have**, has) an uncle.
4. They (**have**, has) two sisters.
5. (**Do**, Does) you (**have**, has) any cousin?

B 1. I have a big family of **forty**.
2. My grandmother is **one hundred** years old.
3. Jim has **fifteen** cousins.
4. **Sixty-five** children are having dinner together.
5. They have **thirty-five**-year-old daughter.

C 1. are they / They are / What are their / Their names are / are they / is twenty / is twenty-two
2. is he / He is / What is his / His name is / is he / He's nineteen

❸ CONVERSATION

B 1. Does he have nephews / he doesn't
2. Do they have nieces / they do / They have three nieces
3. Does she have a cousin / she doesn't
4. Do your parents have brothers / they do / They have four brothers
5. Does Sophie have children / she does / She has two children

Out to the world with Mr. Moon

A Vocabulary

father 아버지   mother 어머니   husband 남편   wife 아내   parents 부모님
children 아이들   son 아들   daughter 딸   brother 형제   sister 자매
grandfather 할아버지   grandmother 할머니   grandchildren 손자, 손녀
grandson 손자   granddaughter 손녀   uncle 삼촌   aunt 고모, 이모   niece 여자조카
nephew 남자조카   cousin 사촌   both 둘 다

B Reading
1. James has a (**big**, small) family.
2. James has (**one**, no) brother.
3. Fred is James' (niece, **nephew**).
4. His father has two (**brothers**, uncles).
5. Joe is James' (cousin, **uncle**).
6. Maggie is James' (sister, **aunt**).
7. Julie is James' (**cousin**, aunt).

Unit 5 I go bungee jumping on Saturday.

② GRAMMAR

A
1. What time is it?
2. What month is it?
3. What is the date?
4. What year is it?
5. What day is it?

B 1. at   2. on   3. on   4. in   5. on   6. at   7. in

C
1. A: Does Mary exercise on Mondays?
   B: No, she doesn't.
   A: What does she do on Mondays?
   B: She goes singing.
2. A: Do you clean your room on Fridays?
   B: No, I don't.
   A: What do you do on Fridays?
   B: I go dancing.
3. A: Does Mike wash his car on Tuesdays?
   B: No, he doesn't.
   A: What does he do on Tuesdays?
   B: He goes bungee jumping.
4. A: Do your parents play tennis on Wednesdays?
   B: No, they don't.
   A: What do they do on Wednesdays?
   B: They go hiking.
5. A: Does Tom study on Thursdays?
   B: No, he doesn't.
   A: What does he do on Thursdays?
   B: He goes camping.

③ CONVERSATION

B
1. A: What <u>does</u> Mandy do on weekdays?
   B: <u>She works.</u>
   A: What <u>does she</u> do on Sundays?
   B: <u>She surfs the Internet.</u>
2. A: What <u>do</u> Jeff and Kathy do on weekdays?
   B: <u>They go to school.</u>
   A: What <u>do they</u> do on Sundays?
   B: <u>They go to the movies.</u>
3. A: What <u>do</u> you and your sister do on weekdays?
   B: <u>We go to work.</u>
   A: What <u>do you</u> do on Sundays?
   B: <u>We do yoga.</u>
4. A: What <u>do</u> your friends do on weekdays?
   B: <u>They study.</u>
   A: What <u>do they</u> do on Sundays?
   B: <u>They have a drink.</u>
5. A: What <u>does</u> George do on weekdays?
   B: <u>He baby-sits.</u>
   A: What <u>does he</u> do on Sundays?
   B: <u>He sleeps all day long.</u>

Out to the world with Mr. Moon

A Vocabulary

Sunday 일요일   Monday 월요일   Tuesday 화요일   Wednesday 수요일   Thursday 목요일
Friday 금요일   Saturday 토요일   January 1월   February 2월   March 3월
April 4월   May 5월   June 6월   July 7월   August 8월
September 9월   October 10월   November 11월   December 12월   baby-sit 아기를 봐 주다
bungee jump 번지 점프하다   clean 청소하다   do yoga 요가하다   fish 생선, 낚시하다
go ~ing ~하러 가다   have a drink 술을 마시다   play tennis 테니스 치다   scuba dive 스쿠버 다이브
surf the Internet 인터넷 검색하다

B Reading

1. a   2. b   3. a   4. b   5. a   6. b   7. b

Unit 6 My favorite sport is soccer.

❷ GRAMMAR

A 1. like   2. like   3. likes   4. like   5. like   6. likes

B 1. sports does he / He likes baseball
2. flowers do Carol and Josh / They like roses
3. books does Marilyn / She likes comic books
4. movies do you / I like science fiction movies

C 1. A: Who's your favorite actor?
  B: My favorite actor is Tom Cruise.
2. A: What's your favorite book?
  B: My favorite book is the Harry Potter series.
3. A: What's your favorite sport?
  B: My favorite sport is basketball.
4. A: Who's your favorite soccer player?
  B: My favorite soccer player is Beckham.
5. A: What's your favorite drama?
  B: My favorite drama is the Big Bang Theory.
6. A: What's your favorite movie?
  B: My favorite movie is Forrest Gump.

❸ CONVERSATION

B 1. What's your favorite movie?
2. What's your favorite book?
3. What's your favorite animal?
4. What's your favorite music?
5. What's your favorite food?

C 1. A: Do you like <u>books</u>?
  B: Of course. I love <u>books</u>. How about you?
  A: Me, too. My favorite <u>book</u> is <u>Hamlet</u>.
2. A: Do you like <u>sports</u>?
  B: Of course. I love <u>sports</u>. How about you?
  A: Me, too. My favorite <u>sport</u> is <u>football</u>.
3. A: Do you like <u>fruits</u>?
  B: Of course. I love <u>fruits</u>. How about you?
  A: Me, too. My favorite <u>fruit</u> is <u>an orange</u>.
4. A: Do you like <u>music</u>?
  B: Of course. I love <u>music</u>. How about you?
  A: Me, too. My favorite <u>music</u> is <u>rock music</u>.
5. A: Do you like <u>movies</u>?
  B: Of course. I love <u>movies</u>. How about you?
  A: Me, too. My favorite <u>movie</u> is <u>About Time</u>.

Out to the world with Mr. Moon

A Vocabulary

romantic comedy 로맨틱 코미디   western 서부극   science fiction movie 공상과학 영화
horror movie 공포영화   comic book 만화책   novel 소설   poetry 시   biography 전기
classical music 고전음악   pop music 대중음악   jazz 재즈   rock music 록음악   baseball 야구
basketball 농구   football 미식축구   golf 골프   soccer 축구   volleyball 배구
favorite 가장 좋아하는   kind 종류   player 선수, 연주자   snake 뱀

B Reading
1. Yes, she does.
2. Her favorite animal is a dog.
3. No, she walks it every morning.
4. Her favorite color is pink.
5. No, her favorite color is yellow.
6. No, she doesn't wear it.
7. No, he likes rock music.
8. His favorite thing is his T-shirt.

Unit 7 I usually drink coffee five times a day.

2 GRAMMAR

A
1. Sheena usually goes swimming on Fridays.
2. My parents sometimes help me with my homework.
3. David never eats chocolate.
4. Do you often go to the movies?
5. Kelly rarely eats lettuce.

B
1. Morris is sometimes angry.
2. We are often tired.
3. Too much caffeine is rarely good for you.
4. My neighbors are sometimes noisy.
5. Cats are rarely friendly.
6. Matt is usually good at English.

C
1. No, I rarely go to work by bus. I usually go to work by subway.
2. No, she sometimes exercises in the morning. She usually exercises in the evening.
3. No, my family rarely eats out on Saturdays. My family usually eats out on Sundays.
4. No, he never drinks coffee at night. He usually drinks coffee in the morning.
5. No, he sometimes reads the newspaper in the bathroom. He usually reads the newspaper in the living room.
6. No, she is never quiet. She is usually talkative.

3 CONVERSATION

B
1. A: How often does your husband have a drink?
   B: He has a drink twice a week.
2. A: How often is Alan late for school?
   B: He is late for school every day.
3. A: How often do you brush your teeth?
   B: I brush my teeth three times a day.
4. A: How often do they go to the gym?
   B: They go to the gym four times a week.
5. A: How often does your brother clean his room?
   B: He cleans his room once a year.

C
1. A: I usually eat fried chicken four times a week.
   B: Four times a week? Well, you eat too much.
      I rarely eat fried chicken
2. A: I usually read books 10 hours a day.
   B: 10 hours a day? Well, you read too much.
      I rarely read books.
3. A: I usually have soda five times a day.
   B: Five times a day? Well, you have too much.
      I rarely have soda.
4. A: I usually spend time at work 12 hours a day.
   B: 12 hours a day? Well, you spend too much.
      I rarely spend time at work.
5. A: I usually have meat seven times a week.
   B: Seven times a week? Well, you have too much.
      I rarely have meat.

Out to the world with Mr. Moon

A Vocabulary

always 언제나	usually 대개	often 종종	sometimes 가끔	rarely 거의~않다
never 결코~않다	eat out 외식하다	friendly 사교적인, 친밀한	fruit 과일	give up 포기하다
kind 친절한	part-time job 아르바이트		talkative 수다스러운	vegetable 채소

B Reading

1. Chuck (usually, **rarely**) gets up early.
2. He usually (**eats**, doesn't eat) breakfast.
3. He always goes to school by (**subway**, bus).
4. He is (**sometimes**, rarely) late for school.
5. He usually (sees his friends, **goes to work**) after school.
6. He works (**five times**, three times) a week.
7. He is (always, **often**) tired.
8. He is never (**unhappy**, happy).

Unit 8 It's raining a lot today.

② GRAMMAR

A 1 - c   2 – d   3 – a   4 – e   5 – b

B 1. I want to have this bag.
2. Angela wants to take a vacation.
3. Do you want to wear those blue jeans?
4. We want to drink some milk.

C 1. A: What's the weather like in <u>Tokyo</u>?
   B: <u>It's cold</u>. How's the weather in <u>Sydney</u>?
   A: It's <u>warm</u>.
2. A: What's the weather like in <u>Hong Kong</u>?
   B: <u>It's raining</u>. How's the weather in <u>Toronto</u>?
   A: It's <u>snowing</u>.
3. A: What's the weather like in <u>London</u>?
   B: It's <u>foggy</u>. How's the weather in <u>Shanghai</u>?
   A: It's <u>windy</u>.
4. A: What's the weather like in <u>Boston</u>?
   B: <u>It's freezing</u>. How's the weather in <u>Athens</u>?
   A: <u>It's humid</u>.
5. A: What's the weather like in <u>Paris</u>?
   B: <u>It's cool</u>. How's the weather in <u>Berlin</u>?
   A: <u>It's chilly</u>.

③ CONVERSATION

B 1. A: How's the weather today? Is it <u>warm</u>?
   B: No, it's still <u>cold</u>.
   A: I hate <u>cold</u> weather.
2. A: How's the weather today? Is it <u>sunny</u>?
   B: No, it's still <u>rainy</u>.
   A: I hate <u>rainy</u> weather.
3. A: How's the weather today? Is it <u>dry</u>?
   B: No, it's still <u>humid</u>.
   A: I hate <u>humid</u> weather.
4. A: How's the weather today? Is it <u>warm</u>?
   B: No, it's still <u>chilly</u>.
   A: I hate <u>chilly</u> weather.
5. A: How's the weather today? Is it <u>cool</u>?
   B: No, it's still <u>steamy</u>.
   A: I hate <u>steamy</u> weather.

Out to the world with Mr. Moon

A Vocabulary

awesome 굉장한, 멋진	Celsius 섭씨	chilly 쌀쌀한	cloudy 흐린	cold 추운
cool 시원한	degree 도(기온)	excellent 훌륭한	fall (= autumn) 가을	Fahrenheit 화씨
foggy 안개 낀	hot 더운	humid 습한	rainy (raining) 비가 오는	
snowy (snowing) 눈이 오는	spring 봄	still 여전히	steamy 푹푹 찌는	summer 여름
sunny 맑은	table tennis 탁구	temperature 기온	warm 따뜻한	weather 날씨
windy 바람 부는	winter 겨울			

B Reading
<u>F</u> 1. It's cloudy.
<u>F</u> 2. He's at school now.
<u>T</u> 3. He's doesn't have an umbrella.
<u>T</u> 4. He wants to have hot chocolate.
<u>F</u> 5. He likes summer.
<u>F</u> 6. His favorite season is summer.
<u>F</u> 7. We have colorful leaves in winter.
<u>T</u> 8. He's looking forward to autumn.

Unit 9 Can you ride a bicycle?

2 GRAMMAR

A
1. I can't in-line skate
2. she can sing a song
3. he can stand on his head
4. Jack can't solve the problem
5. she can drive a car

B
1. A: Can Jane speak English?
   B: No, she can't but she can speak French.
2. A: Can you ride a motorcycle?
   B: No, I can't but I can ride a bicycle.
3. A: Can they play baseball?
   B: No, they can't but they can play basketball.
4. A: Can Bill ski?
   B: No, he can't but he can skate.
5. A: Can Mr. Moor read Chinese characters?
   B: No, he can't but he can read the Korean alphabet.

C
1. They're good at speaking Japanese.
2. He's good at playing tennis.
3. He's good at painting pictures.
4. Betty's good at baking apple pies.
5. They're good at dancing.

3 CONVERSATION

B
1. A: Wow! You can play the drums very well.
   B: Thanks. Can you play the drums, too?
   A: No, I can't play them.
2. A: Wow! You can bake cakes very well.
   B: Thanks. Can you bake cakes, too?
   A: No, I can't bake them.
3. A: Wow! You can ride a horse very well.
   B: Thanks. Can you ride a horse, too?
   A: No, I can't ride it.
4. A: Wow! You can make sandwiches very well.
   B: Thanks. Can you make sandwiches, too?
   A: No, I can't make them.
5. A: Wow! You can fix a car very well.
   B: Thanks. Can you fix a car, too?
   A: No, I can't fix it.

C
1. A: Can Jack fix radios?
   B: Of course. He's pretty good at fixing radios.
2. A: Can you cut hair?
   B: Of course. I am pretty good at cutting hair.
3. A: Can Josh and Bruce play table tennis?
   B: Of course. They're pretty good at playing table tennis.
4. A: Can Lindsay paint houses?
   B: Of course. She's pretty good at painting houses.
5. A: Can Brian speak Chinese?
   B: Of course. He's good at speaking Chinese.

Out to the world with Mr. Moon

A Vocabulary

athletic 운동을 잘 하는	bake 굽다	be good at ~을 잘하다	Chinese characters 한자	cook 요리하다
dance 춤추다	drive a car 차를 운전하다		fix a car 차를 고치다	paint 그림을 그리다
ride a bicycle 자전거를 타다		play the piano 피아노를 연주하다	physical education teacher 체육 선생님	
sing 노래하다	skate 스케이트를 타다		ski 스키를 타다	various 다양한

B Reading

1. They're looking for a job.
2. She can act, sing, dance, and play musical instruments.
3. She can play the piano, the guitar, and the drums.
4. She wants to be a musical singer.
5. Yes, she does.
6. No, she's good at all sports.
7. Yes, she can.
8. She wants to be a physical education teacher.

Unit 10 Can I have French fries?

2 GRAMMAR

A 1 – e   2 – d   3 – f   4 – a   5 – b   6 – c

B 1. Does Molly (have to, has to) leave now?
2. My brother (have to, has to) see a doctor.
3. Jim has to (washes, wash) his clothes.
4. What (do, does) he have to do today?
5. You have to (be, are) quiet in public places.

C 1. you can't / You have to study hard.
2. you can't / You have to get up early.
3. we can't / We have to wait for thirty minutes.
4. you can't / You have to make money.
5. you can't / You have to save money.

3 CONVERSATION

B 1. A: Can I have a hamburger?
     B: No, you can't. You have to eat a salad.
2. A: Can I go to the movies?
     B: No, you can't. You have to take care of the babies.
3. A: Can I go to Henry's party?
     B: No, you can't. You have to clean your room.
4. A: Can I have some cake?
     B: No, you can't. You have to lose weight.
5. A: Can I go to a soccer game?
     B: No, you can't. You have to go to the dentist.

Out to the world with Mr. Moon

A Vocabulary

answer the phone 전화를 받다   clean the room 방을 청소하다   drive a car 차를 운전하다
go to a party 파티에 가다   go to a soccer game 축구경기에 가다   go to the dentist 치과에 가다
go to the movies 영화 보러 가다   make a sandwich 샌드위치를 만들다   pass ~ pepper ~에게 후추를 건네주다
see a doctor 진찰을 받다

B Reading

1. Jessica has three **children**.
2. She **has to** get up early in the morning.
3. She **has to** make breakfast.
4. She **drives her children** to school.
5. She **has to help her children** do their homework.
6. Her children come home **in the afternoon**.
7. She **is very busy every day**.

Appendixes

Grammar Summary

Unit 1

Be + Descriptive Adjectives					
Questions		Answers			
Am I Are you Is he/she/it Are we Are they	thin?	Yes,	you are. I am. he/she is. we are. they are.	No,	you aren't. I am (= I'm) not. he/she/it isn't. we aren't. they aren't.

Or Question
Am I thin or heavy? - You're thin.

Unit 2

Present Continuous (Be + Base verb + ing)			
Statements		Questions	
I'm You're He's/She's/It's We're They're	working.	Am I Are you Is he/she/it Are we Are they	working?
Short Answers			
Yes,	you are. I am. he/she/it is. we are. they are.	No,	you aren't. I'm not. he/she/it isn't. we aren't. they aren't.

Unit 3

This, These, That, Those + Singular/Plural Nouns	
Singular	Plural
This is a shirt.	These are shirts.
That is a shirt.	Those are shirts.
This shirt is on sale.	These shirts are on sale.
That shirt is on sale.	Those shirts are on sale.

Pronunciations of Plural Nouns

[s]: shirts, hats, coats (most nouns)

[z]: shoes, jeans, gloves (nouns ending in a, e, i, o, u, l, m, n, r)

[iz]: blouses, boxes, watches (nouns ending in s, x, z, sh, ch)

Unit 4

Have/Has

Affirmative		Questions			Short Answers			
I You We They	have a brother.	Do	I you we they	have a brother?	Yes,	I do. you do. we do. they do.	No,	I don't. you don't. we don't. they don't.
He She	has a brother.	Does	He She			he does. she does.		he doesn't. she doesn't.

Unit 5

What + Noun + Be + It? / on, in, at (prepositions of time)

Questions		Answers	
What	day is it? month is it? year is it? time is it? is the date?	It's	Sunday. September. 2015. 6 o'clock. September 1st (the first of September).

Prepositions of Time

on + day / date: on Sunday / on September 1st   at + time: at 6 o'clock
in + month / year: in September / in 2015

Unit 6

Like + Noun

Statements	Questions
I / you / we / they like soccer. He / She / It likes soccer.	Do I / you / we / they like soccer? Does he / she / it like soccer?
Answers	
Yes, I / you / we / they do. Yes, he / she / it does.	No, I / you / we / they don't. No, he / she / it doesn't.

What kind(s) of + noun + do you like?: What kinds of sports do you like?
What kind of music do you like?
What is your favorite + noun?: What is your favorite sport?

Grammar Summary 103

Unit 7

Frequency Adverbs	
Questions	Answers (Subject + Frequency Adverb + Verb)
How often do I drink coffee?	You always drink coffee.
How often do you drink coffee?	I usually drink coffee.
How often does he drink coffee?	He often drinks coffee.
How often does she drink coffee?	She sometimes drinks coffee.
How often do we drink coffee?	We rarely drink coffee.
How often do they drink coffee?	They never drink coffee.

Subject + Be + Frequency Adverb

: Coffee is always (usually, often, sometimes, rarely, never) good for you.

The Number of Times

: I drink coffee once (twice, three times, four times, five times…) a day.

Unit 8

Want to + Base verb / It (Pronoun: Impersonal Subject)	
Statements	Questions
I / You / We / They want to play tennis. He / She wants to play tennis.	Do I / you / we / they want to play tennis? Does he / she want to play tennis?
Questions	Answers
What's the weather like?	It's sunny / cloudy / rainy / windy / snowy.
How's the weather?	It's hot / warm / cool / cold.
What's the temperature?	It's 20℃ (= twenty degrees Celsius).
	It's 50°F (= fifty degrees Fahrenheit).
What season is it?	It's spring / summer / fall / winter.

Unit 9

Can (Ability) + Base verb			
Statements		**Questions**	
I You He/She We They	can ride a bicycle.	Can	I You He/She We They	ride a bicycle?
Answers			
Yes,	I can. you can. he/she can. we can. they can.	No,	I can't. you can't. he/she can't. we can't. they can't.

be good at + noun
I'm good at mathematics.

be good at + ~ing(base verb+ing)
I'm good at riding a bicycle.

Unit 10

Can (Permission / Request)			
	Questions	**Polite Questions**	**Answers**
Permission	Can I have French fries?	Could I have French fries?	Yes, you can. No, you can't.
Request	Can you help me?	Could you help me?	Yes, I can. No, I can't.

Have (Has) to + Base verb	
Statements	**Questions**
I / You / We / They have to go. He / She / It has to go.	Do I / you / we / they have to go? Does he / she / it have to go?

Vocabulary Summary

Unit 1

young/new - old 젊은 / 새로운 – 늙은 / 오래된
married - single 결혼한 – 미혼의
beautiful/pretty - ugly 아름다운/예쁜 – 못생긴
noisy - quiet 시끄러운 – 조용한
curly - straight 곱슬곱슬한 – 직모의
strong - weak 힘이 센 – 약한
different 다른

heavy/fat - thin 무거운/살찐 – 마른
handsome - ugly 잘생긴 – 못생긴
large/big - small/little 큰 – 작은
rich - poor 부유한 – 가난한
fair-skinned - dark-skinned (피부가) 흰 – 거무스름한
active - shy 활동적인 – 수줍은
good-looking 외모가 준수한, 예쁜

Unit 2

cooking 요리하고 있는
playing 놀고 (연주하고) 있는
swimming 수영하고 있는

drinking 마시고 있는
reading 읽고 있는
watching 지켜보고 있는

driving 운전하고 있는
singing 노래하고 있는
working 일하고 있는

eating 먹고 있는
sleeping 자고 있는
talking on the phone 전화 통화하고 있는

listening 듣고 있는
studying 공부하고 있는

Unit 3

belt 벨트
earrings 귀걸이
jacket 상의
purse 핸드백
steal 공짜, 훔치다

blouse 블라우스
glasses 안경
jeans 청바지
shirt 셔츠
sweater 스웨터

boots 장화
gloves 장갑
on sale 세일 중
shoes 신발
tie 넥타이

coat 코트
hat 모자
pajamas 잠옷
skirt 치마
wear 입다

dress 옷, 원피스
half price 반값
pants 바지
socks 양말

Unit 4

father 아버지
children 아이들
grandfather 할아버지
grandson 손자
nephew 남자조카

mother 어머니
son 아들
grandmother 할머니
granddaughter 손녀
cousin 사촌

husband 남편
daughter 딸
grandchildren 손자, 손녀
uncle 삼촌
both 둘 다

wife 아내
brother 형제

aunt 고모, 이모

parents 부모님
sister 자매

niece 여자조카

Unit 5

Sunday 일요일
Friday 금요일
April 4월
September 9월
bungee jump 번지 점프하다
go ~ing ~하러 가다
surf the Internet 인터넷 검색하다

Monday 월요일
Saturday 토요일
May 5월
October 10월
clean 청소하다
have a drink 술을 마시다

Tuesday 화요일
January 1월
June 6월
November 11월
do yoga 요가하다
play tennis 테니스 치다

Wednesday 수요일
February 2월
July 7월
December 12월
fish 생선, 낚시하다
scuba dive 스쿠버 다이브

Thursday 목요일
March 3월
August 8월
baby-sit 아기를 봐 주다

Unit 6

romantic comedy 로맨틱 코미디
horror movie 공포영화
classical music 고전음악
basketball 농구
favorite 가장 좋아하는

western 서부극
comic book 만화책
pop music 대중음악
football 미식축구
kind 종류

science fiction movie 공상과학 영화
novel 소설
jazz 재즈
golf 골프
player 선수, 연주자

poetry 시
rock music 록음악
soccer 축구
snake 뱀

biography 전기
baseball 야구
volleyball 배구

Unit 7

always 언제나
never 결코~않다
kind 친절한

usually 대개
eat out 외식하다
part-time job 아르바이트

often 종종
friendly 사교적인, 친밀한

sometimes 가끔
fruit 과일
talkative 수다스러운

rarely 거의~않다
give up 포기하다
vegetable 채소

Unit 8

awesome 굉장한, 멋진
cool 시원한
foggy 안개 낀
snowy (snowing) 눈이 오는
sunny 맑은
windy 바람 부는

Celsius 섭씨
degree 도(기온)
hot 더운
spring 봄
table tennis 탁구
winter 겨울

chilly 쌀쌀한
excellent 훌륭한
humid 습한
still 여전히
temperature 기온

cloudy 흐린
fall (= autumn) 가을
rainy (raining) 비가 오는
steamy 푹푹 찌는
warm 따뜻한

cold 추운
Fahrenheit 화씨
summer 여름
weather 날씨

Unit 9

athletic 운동을 잘 하는
dance 춤추다
ride a bicycle 자전거를 타다
sing 노래하다

bake 굽다
drive a car 차를 운전하다
skate 스케이트를 타다

be good at ~을 잘하다
play the piano 피아노를 연주하다

Chinese characters 한자
fix a car 차를 고치다
physical education teacher 체육 선생님
ski 스키를 타다

cook 요리하다
paint 그림을 그리다
various 다양한

Unit 10

answer the phone 전화를 받다
go to a party 파티에 가다
go to the movies 영화 보러 가다
see a doctor 진찰을 받다

clean the room 방을 청소하다
go to a soccer game 축구경기에 가다
make a sandwich 샌드위치를 만들다

drive a car 차를 운전하다
go to the dentist 치과에 가다
pass ~ pepper ~에게 후추를 건네주다

Cardinal · Ordinal Numbers

Cardinal Numbers

1	one	25	twenty-five	1001	one thousand and one
2	two	26	twenty-six	10,000	ten thousand
3	three	27	twenty-seven	100,000	one hundred thousand
4	four	28	twenty-eight	1,000,000	one million
5	five	29	twenty-nine	10,000,000	ten million
6	six	30	thirty	100,000,000	one hundred million
7	seven	31	thirty-one	1,000,000,000	one billion
8	eight	40	forty		
9	nine	41	forty-one		
10	ten	50	fifty		
11	eleven	51	fifty-one		
12	twelve				
13	thirteen	60	sixty		
14	fourteen	61	sixty-one		
15	fifteen	70	seventy		
16	sixteen	71	seventy-one		
17	seventeen	80	eighty		
18	eighteen	81	eighty-one		
19	nineteen	90	ninety		
20	twenty	91	ninety-one		
21	twenty-one				
22	twenty-two	100	one hundred		
23	twenty-three	101	one hundred and one		
24	twenty-four	1000	one thousand		

Ordinal Numbers

1st	first	25th	twenty-fifth	1,000,000th	one millionth
2nd	second	26th	twenty-sixth	10,000,000th	ten millionth
3rd	third	27th	twenty-seventh	100,000,000th	one hundred millionth
4th	fourth	28th	twenty-eighth	1,000,000,000th	one billionth
5th	fifth	29th	twenty-ninth		
6th	sixth	30th	thirtieth		
7th	seventh	31st	thirty-first		
8th	eighth	32nd	thirty-second		
9th	ninth	33rd	thirty-third		
10th	tenth	40th	fortieth		
11th	eleventh	41st	forty-first		
12th	twelfth	42nd	forty-second		
13th	thirteenth	43rd	forty-third		
14th	fourteenth	50th	fiftieth		
15th	fifteenth	60th	sixtieth		
16th	sixteenth	70th	seventieth		
17th	seventeenth	80th	eightieth		
18th	eighteenth	90th	ninetieth		
19th	nineteenth				
20th	twentieth	100th	one hundredth		
21st	twenty-first	101st	one hundred-and-first		
22nd	twenty-second	1000th	one thousandth		
23rd	twenty-third	10,000th	ten thousandth		
24th	twenty-fourth	100,000th	one hundred thousandth